# SIMPLY GRILLING WITH MR. BBQ

—⚏—

## BY CHRIS HUGHES

xulon
PRESS

*SIMPLY GRILLING WITH MR. BBQ*
by Chris Hughes

Printed in the United States of America

ISBN 978-1-60034-836-5
ISBN 1-60034-836-X

Unless otherwise indicated, Bible quotations are taken from the King James Version of the Bible.

www.xulonpress.com

# DEDICATION

To my son, Christian Hughes.
You inspire me every day.
I look forward to training you to become the next *Mr. BBQ.*

# TABLE OF CONTENTS

—ᴍ—

# BREADS

—m—

## BOBOLI

### *Grilled Canadian Bacon Boboli*

4 6-inch Boboli bread shells
1 6-ounce jar of marinated artichoke hearts
8 slices of Canadian Bacon, cut into strips
1 cup Mozzarella cheese
2 tomatoes, sliced thinly
½ cup feta cheese
1 green onion, thinly sliced
2 teaspoons chopped oregano

Drain the artichoke hearts and save the juice. Halve the artichoke hearts lengthwise and set aside.

Brush the Boboli breads with the reserve juice, divide the other ingredients and top the pizzas. Wrap the bottoms of each Boboli with heavy duty aluminum foil and place over medium heat on the grill for eight minutes.

# BREAKFAST BREADS

## *Grilled French Toast with Raspberry Sauce*

4 slices of Texas toast
4 eggs
½ to ¾ cup of milk
1 teaspoon of vanilla

**Raspberry Sauce**
2 cups of raspberries
½ cup of honey
2 tablespoons of Grand Marnier or Rum

**Garnish**
Whipped cream
Ground cinnamon
Confectioner's sugar
Mint (optional)

In a medium bowl, mash raspberries. Mix in honey and Grand Marnier and set aside. In a large bowl whip eggs, milk and vanilla. Coat toast evenly in egg mixture and cook on the grill for about 3 to 5 minutes on each side. Place the toast on a platter and pour raspberry mixture over the toast and add two tablespoons of whipped cream in the center and sprinkle with cinnamon and confectioner's sugar. Garnish with a piece of mint.

## *Grilled Ham Biscuits*

1 can of buttermilk biscuits
2 large ham steaks

Placed biscuits in iron skillet sprayed with Pam. Cook over medium heat until cooked and brown. Spray ham steaks with Pam. Grill on medium heat until done, turning often. If you want a little extra flavor, combine equal parts of Ranch salad dressing and Coca-Cola and baste the ham every time that you turn the meat.

## Grilled Sour Cream Muffins

2 cups self-rising flour
2 sticks butter, melted
½ pint sour cream

Preheat grill to medium heat. Combine all ingredients and spoon into small, un-greased muffin tins. Grill for 20 to 30 minutes.

## Grilled Waffles with Raspberry Sauce

1package of frozen waffles (round)
1 container of Cool Whip
16 ounces of raspberries
½ cup of honey
4 tablespoons of Grand Marnier

Mash raspberries with fork. Add honey and Grand Marnier. Grill frozen waffles over medium heat until toasted on each side (about two minutes per side). Place waffles on serving dish, spoon over raspberry sauce, top with whipped cream.

# CORNBREAD

### *Grilled Skillet Cornbread*

¾ cup all purpose flour
¾ cup water
2 ½ teaspoons baking powder
5 tablespoons sugar
1 teaspoon salt
1 ¼ cups yellow corn meal
¼ cup instant nonfat dry milk
1 large egg
3 tablespoons unsalted butter, melted
Vegetable oil for the skillet

Over low heat, heat a 9-inch cast-iron skillet with a cover. Mix flour, baking powder, sugar, salt, cornmeal, and nonfat dry milk in a large bowl. In a small bowl, whisk together egg, ¾ cup water, and melted butter. Make a well in the center of dry ingredients, and pour the egg mixture into it. Stir just until combined.

Brush bottom, sides, and inside of skillet lid with vegetable oil; pour in the batter. Cover, and cook over medium low heat until top feels almost dry, about 35 minutes (check the bottom occasionally to make sure it's not burning; lower heat if necessary).

Transfer to a plate, let cool slightly, and cut into wedges.

## Grilled Southern Cornbread Stuffing

Cornbread (recipe follows)
7 slices oven-dried white bread
1 sleeve saltine crackers
8 tablespoons butter
2 cups celery, chopped
1 large onion, chopped
7 cups chicken stock
1 teaspoon salt
Freshly ground black pepper
1 teaspoon sage (optional)
1 tablespoon poultry seasoning (optional)
5 eggs, beaten

Preheat grill to medium heat.

In a large bowl, combine crumbled cornbread, dried white bread slices, and saltines; set aside.

Melt the butter in a large skillet over medium heat. Add the celery and onion and cook until transparent, approximately 5 to 10 minutes. Pour the vegetable mixture over cornbread mixture. Add the stock, mix well, taste, and add salt, pepper to taste, sage, and poultry seasoning. Add beaten eggs and mix well. Reserve 2 heaping tablespoons of this mixture for the giblet gravy. Pour mixture into a greased cast iron skillet and grill until dressing is cooked through, about 45 minutes.

## Cornbread

1 cup self-rising cornmeal
½ cup self-rising flour
¾ cup buttermilk
2 eggs
2 tablespoons vegetable oil

Preheat grill to medium heat.

Combine all ingredients and mix well. Pour batter into a greased cast iron skillet. Grill for approximately 20 to 25 minutes. Remove from grill and let cool. To serve, cut into desired squares and serve with butter.

# PIZZA

## *Baby Grilled Pizzas*

2 large store-bought pre-baked pizza shells
Your favorite jarred tomato sauce
1 pound grated mozzarella cheese
Grated Pecorino Romano or Parmigiano-Reggiano, as needed
Leaves from 1 large sprig fresh basil

Preheat the grill to medium heat.

Cut rounds from pizza dough using a 2-inch round cutter to make tiny individual crusts. Place pizza rounds on the grill and close the lid for three minutes. Turn the pizza crust over and top with sauce, and cover with mozzarella. Sprinkle a light dusting of grated Pecorino or Parmigiano on top. Grill until cheese is perfectly melted, approximately 7 minutes.

Cut basil leaves into thin strips and sprinkle on top of pizzas with some more grated cheese before serving

## Grilled Pizza with Chicken, Sun-Dried Tomatoes, and Broccoli

### Crust
1 package (16 oz.) pizza dough, brought to room temperature
2 teaspoons extra-virgin olive oil
2 tablespoons grated Parmigiano Reggiano or Parmesan cheese

### Toppings
1/3 pound broccoli
1 tablespoon extra-virgin olive oil
3 cloves garlic, cracked
1/3 pound cooked chicken breast
Salt and freshly ground black pepper, to taste
1 cup part-skim ricotta cheese
10 sun-dried tomatoes in oil, drained and sliced
1 cup shredded mozzarella cheese
12-15 leaves fresh basil, torn or stacked and thinly sliced

On a 12-inch nonstick area, stretch out your dough and form the pizza crust. Drizzle 2 teaspoons olive oil onto crust and spread it with a pastry brush to the edges. Sprinkle crust with grated Parmigiano Reggiano or Parmesan cheese.

In a small covered saucepan, bring 2 inches water to a boil. Separate broccoli tops into florets, discarding lower stalks or reserve for soup. Salt water and add broccoli florets. Cook covered, 3-5 minutes. Drain broccoli, set on cutting board and chop florets into small pieces.

Chop cooked chicken into small pieces.

Heat a very clean grill to medium heat. Spray grate with nonstick cooking spray. Place the dough on the grate. Close the grill lid and grill for five minutes.

Turn the dough and immediately dot crust with chopped broccoli bits, garlic and chicken. Add spoonfuls of ricotta throughout
and spread ricotta gently with the back of your spoon. Add sliced
sun-dried tomatoes, scattering them around the pizza to the edges.
Complete the assembly with a thin layer of shredded mozzarella,
about 1 cup.

Close the lid and grill an additional five minutes. Remove from
the grill and let stand 5 minutes. Top with lots or torn or shredded
basil. Cut pizza into 8 slices, using pizza wheel, and serve.

## Grilled Sicilian Pizza

Boboli bread shell
Plum tomatoes, thinly sliced
1 large red tomato, thinly sliced
4 ounces fresh mozzarella, thinly sliced
1/3 cup pitted kalamata olives
1 tablespoon olive oil
1 cup chopped escarole or endive lettuce
¼ cup Parmesan cheese
Black pepper

Top bread shell with tomatoes, mozzarella cheese and olives.
Drizzle oil all over. Place Boboli on sheet of heavy duty aluminum
foil and fold the edges of the foil over the sides of the bread.

Place on medium heated grill for 8 minutes. Top with the lettuce
the last 2 minutes of grilling. Remove from grill and sprinkle with
shredded cheese and black pepper.

## *Shrimp and Scallops on the Beach Pizza*

24 medium shrimp
12 scallops
1 large fennel, thinly sliced
2 teaspoons olive oil
4 flat breads
½ cup Alfredo sauce
2 cups mozzarella cheese

Peel and de-vein shrimp. Halve scallops. Wash shrimp and scallops and pat dry. Spray grilling wok with non stick cooking spray and grill shrimp and scallops for four minutes and set aside.

Spray both sides of each flat bread with non stick cooking spray. Grill one side for 1 minute. Turn the breads over and drizzle with olive oil. Evenly divide shrimp, scallops, fennel and cheese.

Top each flat bread with Alfredo sauce and place toppings on each pizza. Cover and grill 4-5 minutes, or until cheese melts.

# TOASTS & BREAD

### *Bruschetta with Tomato and Basil*

½ Baguette or crusty long loaf bread
2 large cloves garlic
Extra-virgin olive oil
3 small plum tomatoes
20 fresh basil leaves
Coarse salt

Preheat grill to medium high. Spray bread slices with nonstick cooking spray. Place bread slices on your grill. Toast bread on each side and keep an eye on it! Rub toasts with cracked garlic and drizzle with oil.

Chop seeded tomatoes and place in a small bowl. Pile basil leaves on top of one another and roll into a log. Thinly slice basil into a green confetti and loosely combine with tomatoes. Add a drizzle of oil and a little coarse salt to the bowl and gently toss tomatoes and basil to coat. Place bowl on serving platter with a serving spoon and arrange toasts around the platter.

## Herb and Goat Cheese Toasts

1 Baguette, sliced
Fresh flat-leaf parsley
12 blades fresh chives
2 sprigs fresh rosemary, leaves stripped from stem
Coarse freshly ground black pepper
8 ounces fresh goat cheese

Spray bread with nonstick cooking spray and arrange baguette slices on grill. Toast on grill until lightly golden on each side. Remove and arrange on a serving plate.

Chop and combine fresh chives, rosemary and parsley. Add coarse black pepper to the herb mixture, and then roll goat cheese in the herbs to coat evenly. Set alongside toasts to serve, using a butter knife to spread herbed cheese on warm toasts.

## Bell Pepper Salad and Tomato Toasts

1 onion
2 red bell peppers
2 yellow bell peppers
3 tablespoons olive oil
2 large zucchini, sliced
2 garlic cloves, sliced
1 tablespoon balsamic vinegar
1 ¾ ounces anchovy fillets, chopped
¼ cup black olives, halved and pitted
1 tablespoon chopped fresh basil
Salt and pepper

**Tomato Toasts**
Small stick of French bread
1 Garlic clove, crushed
1 Tomato, peeled and chopped
2 Tablespoons olive oil

Cut the onion into wedges. Core and de-seed the bell peppers and cut into thick slices.

Heat the oil in a large heavy-based skillet. Add the onion, bell peppers, zucchini, and garlic and fry gently for 20 minutes, stirring occasionally. Add the vinegar, anchovies, olives, and seasoning to taste, mix thoroughly and leave to cool.

Spoon on to individual plates and sprinkle with the basil.

To make the tomato toasts, cut the French bread diagonally into ½ inch slices. Mix the garlic, tomato, oil, and seasoning together, and spread thinly over each slice of bread.

Place the bread on a cookie sheet, drizzle with the olive oil and bake in a preheated oven, 425 degrees, for 5-10 minutes until crisp. Serve the Tomato Toasts with the bell pepper salad.

## *Sausage-Stuffed French Bread*

2 15-inch French baguettes
1 pound bulk breakfast sausage
2 tablespoons chopped jalapenos
1 cup chopped green bell peppers
¼ cup chopped green onions (green and white parts)
8 ounces cream cheese, at room temperature
8 ounces sour cream
8 ounces grated sharp Cheddar cheese
1 teaspoon Emeril's Original Essence
Chopped fresh parsley, for garnish
Corn or tortilla chips, for dipping (optional)

### Emeril's Original Essence

1 ½ tablespoons paprika
2 tablespoons salt
2 tablespoons garlic powder
1 tablespoon black pepper
1 tablespoon onion powder
1 tablespoon cayenne pepper
1 tablespoon dried oregano
1 tablespoon dried thyme
1 cup cheddar cheese

Using a serrated knife, trim the upper quarter off the length of the top of each loaf. Hollow out the center of the loaves, leaving a ½-inch thick shell. Set aside.

Brown the sausage in a large skillet over medium-high heat for about 5 minutes, stirring to break up any clumps. Add the jalapenos, bell peppers, and green onions. Cook, stirring, until the vegetables are soft, 3-4 minutes. Add the cream cheese, sour cream, and Cheddar and stir until completely melted, about 2 minutes. Add the Essence and remove from the heat.

Pour the mixture in the bread shell. Sprinkle the top with cheddar cheese. Wrap in foil and grill 5 minutes until the cheese melts. Serve with tortilla chips.

# DRESSINGS & STUFFING

## *Grilled Sausage and Apple Stuffing*

2 sticks plus 3 tablespoons butter, divided
2 cups water
2 large bags of your favorite dried cornbread stuffing mix
1 pound pork sausage (not links)
1 large onion, diced
3 cloves garlic, minced
2 stalks celery, diced
1 teaspoon dried thyme leaves
1 teaspoon dried sage leaves
1 cup chopped walnuts
3 medium apples, cored, sliced

In a large pot melt 2 sticks butter in water. When melted add dry cornbread stuffing stirring to incorporate liquid, set aside.

In a large sauté pan set over medium-high heat, melt 1 tablespoon butter and add sausage. With a wooden spoon break up sausage and sauté until lightly browned and cooked through. Transfer sausage to paper towels to drain.

In the same pan melt remaining butter and sauté onions with the garlic, celery, thyme, and sage until onions are translucent and celery is crisp tender. Add walnuts and sauté for 1 minute.

Add apples and sauté for one minute more. Remove from heat. Combine cornbread stuffing with sautéed ingredients and stuff turkey. Roast turkey as usual. Alternatively fill a 9 x 13 x 2-inch pan with the stuffing and grill at medium heat, covered with foil for thirty minutes. Remove foil and grill until top is lightly browned, about 15 minutes more.

# DESSERTS

## *Apple Crisp*

6 McIntosh apples
The juice of ½ lemon
1 teaspoon ground cinnamon
½ teaspoon nutmeg, ground or fresh
2 tablespoons granulated sugar
½ cup fine graham cracker crumbs
½ cup brown sugar
½ stick butter
1 pint vanilla ice cream

In a mixing bowl, combine apples, lemon juice, cinnamon, nutmeg, and sugar. Spray cast iron skillet with non-stick cooking spray and pour mixture into skillet. In a small bowl, mix graham cracker crumbs, brown sugar, and butter together using the tines of a fork and your fingers, working until small even crumbles form. Sprinkle this mixture evenly over apples and grill 25 to 30 minutes until they are just tender and topping is golden brown. Serve apple crisp with small scoops of vanilla ice cream.

## Autumn Fruit Bread Dessert

4 cups mixed blackberries, chopped apples, chopped pears
¾ cup soft light brown sugar
1 teaspoon cinnamon
8 ounces white bread, thinly sliced, crusts removed (about 12 slices)

Place the fruit in a large saucepan with the soft light brown sugar, cinnamon, and 7 tablespoons of water, stir and bring to a boil. Reduce the heat and simmer for 5-10 minutes so that the fruits soften but still hold their shape.

Meanwhile, line the base and sides of a 3 ¼ cup ovenproof bowl with the bread slices, making sure that there are no gaps between the pieces of bread. Spoon the fruit into the center of the bread-lined bowl and cover the fruit with the remaining bread.

Place a saucer on top of the bread and weigh it down. Chill the dessert in the refrigerator overnight.

Invert the dessert onto a serving plate and serve immediately.

# Barbecued Apples with Crumb Topping

Crumb topping is a favorite on almost any dessert, but wait until
you try it on grilled apples. Use apples that are good for baking
such as Winesap, Rome Beauty or Granny Smith.

## For the topping
½ cup quick-cooking (not instant) oatmeal
½ cup all-purpose flour
½ cup packed light brown sugar
¼ teaspoon ground cinnamon
¼ cup unsalted butter, cut into small pieces
½ cup chopped pecans
4 large baking apples, halved crosswise through the centre, cored
2 tablespoons butter, melted
½ cup heavy cream

*To make the topping:* In a medium bowl combine the oatmeal,
flour, brown sugar, and cinnamon. Add the butter and work it in
evenly with a fork or your fingertips. The crumbles should be the
size of peas. Stir in the pecans. Set aside.

Brush the cut side of the apples with the melted butter. Arrange
the apples cut side down on the grill and cook over direct medium
heat for 20 minutes, turning once halfway through grilling time.
Remove from the grill.

Mound the topping over the cut side of the apples, distributing
evenly. Return apples to the grill and continue grilling over direct
medium heat until the topping is golden brown, about 6 minutes.
Serve warm or at room temperature with the heavy cream drizzled
over the apples.

## *Broiled Fruit Platter*

1 baby pineapple
1 ripe papaya
1 ripe mango
2 kiwi fruit
4 finger bananas
4 tablespoons dark rum
1 teaspoon ground allspice
2 tablespoons lime juice
4 tablespoons dark muscovado sugar

### Lime "Butter"
2 ounces low-fat spread
½ teaspoon finely grated lime rind
1 tablespoon confectioners' sugar

Using a sharp knife, quarter the pineapple, trimming away most of the leaves, and place in a shallow dish. Peel the papaya, cut it in half, and scoop out the seeds. Cut the flesh into thick wedges and place in the same dish as the pineapple.

Peel the mango, cut either side of the smooth, central flat pit and remove the pit. Slice the flesh into thick wedges. Peel the kiwi fruit and cut in half. Peel the bananas. Add all of these fruits to the dish.

Sprinkle over the rum, allspice, and lime juice, cover, and leave at room temperature for 30 minutes, turning occasionally, to allow the flavors to develop.

Meanwhile, make the "butter." Place the low-fat spread in a small bowl and beat in the lime rind and sugar until well mixed. Leave to chill until required.

Preheat the broiler to hot. Drain the fruit, reserving the juices, and arrange in the broiler pan. Sprinkle with the sugar and broil for 3-4 minutes until hot, bubbling, and just beginning to char.

Transfer the fruit to a serving plate and spoon over the juices. Serve with the lime "butter."

## *Chinese Custard Tarts*

### Dough
1 ½ cups all-purpose flour
3 tablespoons superfine sugar
4 tablespoons unsalted butter
2 tablespoons shortening
2 tablespoons water

### Custard
2 small eggs
¼ cup superfine sugar
¾ cup pint milk
½ teaspoon ground nutmeg, plus extra for sprinkling cream, to serve.

To make the dough, sift the all-purpose flour into a bowl. Add the superfine sugar and cut in the butter and shortening until the mixture resembles breadcrumbs. Add the water and mix to form a firm dough.

Transfer the dough to a lightly floured surface and knead for 5 minutes, until smooth. Cover with plastic wrap and leave to chill in the refrigerator while you prepare the filling.

To make the custard, beat the eggs and sugar together. Gradually add the milk and ground nutmeg and beat until well combined.

Separate the dough into 15 even-sized pieces. Flatten the dough pieces into rounds and press into shallow patty pans.

Spoon the custard into the tart shells and cook in a preheated oven at 300 degrees, for 25-30 minutes.

Transfer the Chinese custard tarts to a wire rack, leave to cool slightly, then sprinkle with nutmeg. Serve hot or cold with cream.

## Grilled Banana Sundaes

3 large bananas
1 tablespoon melted butter
2 teaspoons orange juice
½ cup caramel ice cream topping
¼ teaspoon ground cinnamon
1 pint vanilla ice cream
2 tablespoons sliced almond slivers
2 tablespoons shredded coconut

Cut bananas in half, lengthwise. Combine butter and 1 teaspoon orange juice in a bowl. Brush the juice mixture over both sides of each banana and grill over medium heat for four minutes. Turn once.

In a small cast iron skillet, combine the rest of the orange juice, the caramel topping. Heat until it boils and add the cinnamon. Add the bananas to the sauce and coat. Place bananas on a dish. Top with ice cream and the caramel topping mixture. Sprinkle with coconut and almonds.

## *Grilled Fruit Shortcake*

This recipe adds a twist to backyard parties and takes advantage of the fresh fruit that starts to come in during early summer. It is fun to get your guests skewering food, and they will enjoy being part of the show. Have all the fixings and the skewers ready to go. After dinner, set it all out on a table. Have the grill ready to go — cleaned then oiled — and preheated. Your guests can grill their choice of fruit while grilling a slice of cake. This recipe will serve eight. Have a couple of spatulas and several sets of tongs near the grill for the convenience of your guests.

**For the set-up**
Vegetable oil for seasoning the grill grate
8 small bamboo skewers, soaked for at least 20 minutes in water
24 large strawberries
4 ripe but still firm peaches
2 tablespoons balsamic vinegar or lemon juice
1 cup sugar
1 tablespoon cinnamon
1 package commercial pound cake or angel food cake cut in eight slices
Preheat the grill. Prepare the grill grate by cleaning with a wire grill brush then seasoning with vegetable oil.
Rinse strawberries. Cut each peach in half and remove pits. Place peach halves cut side down on a plate coated with balsamic vinegar or lemon juice. Cover peach plate with cling wrap. Refrigerate until dessert time. Mix the sugar and cinnamon and cover.
When it's time to serve, transfer the sugar mixture to a flat dish so that guests can coat their fruit with the sugar mixture before grilling. Set up the fruit and cake on a table outside near the grill. Skewer the strawberries. Place peach halves on the grill top side down and grill for three minutes, turn over and grill for three on the other side. Grill strawberry skewers for one minute on a side. Place cake slices on the grill long enough to heat and get grill marks (about one minute per side). Top each slice of cake with

a peach half and strawberries then top with mascarpone cream (recipe below).

## Mascarpone Cream

8 ounces mascarpone cheese
½ cup confectioner's sugar
½ cup rum, Frangelica, or Amaretto
1 cup heavy cream

With an electric mixer, mix the mascarpone and the liqueur. Add the confectioner's sugar, scraping the sides to mix well. Gradually add the cream and whip to soft peaks. This may be prepared several hours in advance. During dessert prep, keep chilled by placing the bowl over ice.

## Grilled Pears

2 large ripe pears
½ cup white wine
1 tablespoon sugar
1 cinnamon stick (about 2 inches)
½ teaspoon nutmeg
Spray a grill-safe baking dish with cooking spray. Cut pears in half from the top and remove seeds. Place face down in baking dish and cover with remaining ingredients. Cover and place on preheated grill for about 15 minutes.

Remove when most the liquid is gone and pears and easily pierced with a fork.

## Grilled Pears with Raspberry-Grand Marnier Sauce

3 Bosc, Anjou, or other firm winter pears
1 lemon, halved crosswise
¾ cup sugar
1 tablespoon ground cinnamon
1 cup fresh or thawed frozen raspberries
1 teaspoon honey
1 tablespoon Grand Marnier or other orange-flavored liqueur

To make sauce, combine the raspberries and honey in a bowl. Mash the raspberries lightly with a fork and stir in the Grand Marnier. Set aside.

Cut the pears in half lengthwise and remove the cores. Squeeze the lemon over the cut sides of the pears to prevent browning. In a shallow bowl, stir together the sugar and cinnamon. Dip the cut sides of the pears in the cinnamon sugar.

Grill the pears, cut side won, directly over medium-high heat until the fruit is grill-marked and the sugar is caramelized, 2-4 minutes. Do not allow to char. Using a spatula, turn the pears and grill until tender and heated through, 3-4 minutes. If the pears start to char, move them to a cooler part of the grill to cook.

Serve the pears topped with the raspberry sauce and with a scoop of vanilla ice cream alongside, if desired.

## Grilled Pina Colada Pineapple

1 small pineapple
4 tablespoons unsalted butter
2 tablespoons light brown sugar
2/3 cup grated fresh coconut
1 tablespoon rum

Using a very sharp knife, cut the pineapple into quarters and then remove the tough core from the center, leaving the leaves attached. Carefully cut the pineapple flesh away from the skin. Make horizontal cuts across the flesh of the pineapple quarters.

Place the butter in a pan and heat gently until melted, stirring continuously. Brush the melted butter over the pineapple and sprinkle with the sugar. Cover the pineapple leaves with kitchen foil to prevent them from burning, and transfer them to a rack set over the grill.

Grill the pineapple for about 10 minutes. Sprinkle the coconut over the pineapple and broil, cut side up, for 5-10 minutes, or until the pineapple is piping hot.

Transfer the pineapple to serving plates and remove the foil from the leaves. Spoon a little rum over the pineapple and serve at once.

## Grilled Spiced Pecans

4 cups pecan halves
1½ teaspoons Kosher salt
¼ teaspoons cayenne pepper
1 heaping teaspoon dark brown sugar
1 tablespoon melted butter
2 tablespoon olive oil
Pinch of freshly ground black pepper

Place pecans in grilling wok and grill over medium heat for 15 minutes, stirring occasionally. Remove pecans from the grill and season with the salt, pepper, cayenne, sugar, butter, and olive oil. Toss together until pecans are thoroughly coated. Return the pecans to the grill for another 2 to 3 minutes, until toasted and fragrant, but be careful not to overcook them.

## Lemon & Lime Syllabub

¼ cup superfine sugar
Grated rind and juice of 1 small lemon
Grated rind and juice of 1 small lime
¼ cup Marsala or medium sherry
1 ¼ cups heavy cream
Lime and lemon rind, to decorate

Put the sugar, lemon juice and rind, lime juice and rind, and sherry in a bowl, mix well, and set aside to infuse for 2 hours.

Add the cream to the fruit juice mixture and whisk until it just holds its shape. Spoon the mixture into 4 tall serving glasses and chill in the refrigerator for 2 hours.

Decorate with lime and lemon rind and serve.

## Panettone & Strawberries

8 ounces strawberries
2 tablespoons superfine sugar
6 tablespoons Marsala wine
½ teaspoon ground cinnamon
4 slices panettone
4 tablespoons mascarpone cheese

Hull and slice the strawberries and place them in a bowl. Add the sugar, Marsala, and cinnamon to the strawberries. Toss the strawberries in the sugar and cinnamon mixture until they are well coated. Leave to chill in the refrigerator for at least 30 minutes.

When ready to serve, transfer the slices of panettone to a medium heated grill. Grill the panettone for about 1 minute on each side or until golden brown. Carefully remove the panettone from the grill and transfer to serving plates

Top the panettone with the mascarpone cheese and the marinated strawberries.

# Pound Cake Kabobs with Chocolate-Coffee Sauce

**Chocolate-coffee sauce**
4 ounce unsweetened chocolate, chopped
¼ cup unsalted butter
1 cup sugar
½ cup evaporated milk
2 tablespoons coffee liqueur
1 teaspoon vanilla extract

6 slices pound cake, each 1 inch
3 bananas, peeled and cut into 1-inch lengths
Melted unsalted butter for brushing
Whipped cream

Prepare a medium heated grill.

To prepare the sauce, combine the chocolate and butter in the top pan of a double boiler or in a heatproof bowl. Place over (not touching) simmering water in a pan. Stir until smooth.

Using a rubber spatula, scrape the chocolate mixture into a clean saucepan. Stir in the sugar and evaporated milk and bring to a simmer over medium-high heat, stirring until the sugar dissolves and the sauce is heated through. Stir in the liqueur and vanilla and remove from the heat.

Thread the cake and banana pieces alternately onto 6 skewers, dividing them evenly. Brush with the butter, place on the grill rack, and grill, turning once, until the cake is lightly toasted, about 2 minutes total.

Gently re-warm the chocolate sauce over low heat. Pour a pool of the sauce onto 6 individual plates, dividing evenly. Add a dollop of whipped cream, if desired. Place 1 skewer on each plate, drizzle with some of the warmed sauced, and serve hot.

## *Rhubarb & Orange Crumble*

1 pound 2 ounces rhubarb
1 pound 2 ounces cooking apples
Grated rind and juice of 1 orange
1 teaspoon ground cinnamon
Scant ½ cup light soft brown sugar

### Crumble
2 cups Graham cracker
½ cup butter or margarine
Generous ½ cup light soft brown sugar
½ cup toasted chopped hazelnuts
2 tablespoons brown crystal sugar

Cut the rhubarb into 1-inch lengths and place in a large saucepan.

Peel, core, and slice the apples and add to the rhubarb, together with the grated orange rind and juice. Bring to a boil on the grill side burner, lower the heat, and simmer for 2-3 minutes, until the fruit begins to soften. Add the cinnamon and sugar to taste and transfer the mixture to a grill proof dish, so it is not more than two-thirds full.

Sift the flour into a bowl and cut in the butter or margarine until the mixture resembles fine breadcrumbs (this can be done by hand or in a food processor). Stir in the sugar, followed by the nuts.

Spoon the crumble mixture evenly over the fruit in the dish and level the top. Sprinkle with brown crystal sugar, if like.

Grill in a preheated grill over medium heat for 30-40 minutes, until the topping is browned. Serve hot or cold.

## Spicy Grilled Nuts

Assorted shelled nuts (almonds, cashews, peanuts, etc.)

**For sweet and spicy nuts**
Peanut oil, for drizzling
Sugar, to taste
Kosher salt, to taste
Chinese five-spice powder, to taste
**For savory nuts**
Peanut oil, for drizzling
Kosher salt, to taste
Chili powder, to taste
Preheat the grill to medium high heat.

For a sweet and spicy nut, toss your choice of nuts with oil, sugar, salt and a few dashes of Chinese five-spice powder.
For a savory and spicy nut, toss your choice of nuts with oil, salt and a few dashes of chili powder.
Lay out the nuts in an even layer on a grilling pan. Grill, redistributing the nuts every 7 minutes or so to make sure they cook evenly, until the nuts are lightly browned, about 15 to 20 minutes.

# MEATS

—⁓—

## BEEF

### *Beer-Marinated Peppered T-Bones*

1 cup chopped onion
½ of a 12-ounce can ( ¾ cup) beer
¾ cup chili sauce
¼ cup parsley
3 tablespoons Dijon-style mustard
1 tablespoon Worcestershire sauce
2 teaspoons brown sugar
½ teaspoon paprika
½ teaspoon ground black pepper
3 beef T-bone steaks, cut 1-inch thick (about 1 pound each), or 6
beef top loin steaks, cut 1-inch thick (about 1 ¾ pounds total)
1 to 1 ½ teaspoons cracked black pepper
Fresh herbs (optional)

In a large glass baking dish combine onion, beer, chili sauce,
parsley, mustard, Worcestershire sauce, brown sugar, paprika, and
½ teaspoon pepper. Place steaks in marinade. Cover and refrigerate
4-6 hours or overnight, turning steaks over occasionally.

Remove steaks from marinade; discard marinade. Sprinkle both
sides of steaks with the cracked black pepper.

Grill steaks on an uncovered grill directly over medium high heat
for 5 minutes. Turn and grill to desired doneness, allowing 7-10
minutes more for medium (160 degrees F) doneness. If desired,
garnish with fresh herbs.

## Delmonico Steaks with Balsamic Onions and Steak Sauce

4 Delmonico steaks, 1-inch thick (10-12 oz)
Montreal Seasoning, to taste

Sprinkle steaks with steak seasoning. Spray with nonstiick cooking spray and grill over medium heat for 3 minutes on each side. Separate half of the steak sauce. Baste with the steak sauce. Remove from grill. Top with onions and steak sauce and serve.

### Onions
1 tablespoon extra-virgin olive oil
2 large yellow onions, thinly sliced
¼ cup balsamic vinegar

Place the olive oil in a cast iron skillet and heat to medium heat on your side burner. Add onions and sauté for 2 minutes. Add the balsamic vinegar and simmer for 8 more minutes.

### Steak Sauce
1 ½ teaspoons extra-virgin olive oil
2 cloves garlic, chopped
1 small white boiling onion, chopped
¼ cup dry cooking sherry
1 cup canned tomato sauce
1 tablespoon Worcestershire sauce
Black pepper to taste

Place the olive oil in a cast iron skillet and heat to medium heat on your side burner. Add onions and garlic and sauté for 2 minutes. Add remaining ingredients and sautéed for 7 minutes.

## *Grilled Mini Hamburgers with Onion Relish*

1 pound ground sirloin
½ pound ground pork
½ pound ground veal
Salt and freshly ground pepper
1 tablespoon extra-virgin olive oil
Rolls
16 dill pickles
Onion Relish, recipe follows

Heat grill to high.

Combine all of the ground meat into a large mixing bowl. Shape into 16 (1-ounce) patties. Season patties generously with salt and pepper and drizzle with oil.

Cook burgers on a very hot grill for about 30 seconds on each side. Serve the patties on rolls garnished with a dill pickle and Onion Relish.

**Onion Relish**
2 tablespoons extra-virgin olive oil
3 cloves garlic
2 onions, cut in half lengthwise and sliced thinly
Salt and freshly ground pepper
½ cup water
½ cup ketchup
2 tablespoons yellow mustard
 Heat a large skillet over medium-high heat on the grill and add the olive oil and garlic cloves. Sauté the garlic until lightly browned. Add the onions and continue to cook the mixture until golden brown. Season well with salt and pepper, add the water, stir, and bring to a boil, scraping up the caramelized bits on the bottom of the pan. Stir in ketchup and mustard. Simmer until thick. Remove from heat and let cool before serving with the burgers.

## Gold Miner's Grilled Chili

1 ½ cup minced grilled onion
4 tablespoons minced garlic
2 cans chicken broth
4 ounces tomato sauce
¾ teaspoon garlic powder
3 tablespoons ground cumin
10 ½ tablespoons chili powder
2 teaspoons salt
3 pounds of grilled steak, cut into ¼ inch cubes
½ teaspoon Accent
½ teaspoon light brown sugar
1 teaspoon hot red pepper sauce

In a large pot, mix chopped grilled onions, the minced garlic and two cups of chicken broth. Simmer on the grill for ten minutes. Add the tomato sauce and all of the dry spices, except the meat tenderizer, pepper sauce and the brown sugar.

Sprinkle the steak with the meat tenderizer, prior to grilling. Grill to medium doneness. Cut the meat into ¼ inch cubes. Add to the chili pot. Add remaining broth and simmer for 1 ½ hours.

Mix in brown sugar and hot sauce just before serving.

You may want to serve the chili with Fritos, sour cream, shredded cheese, and jalapeno peppers.

## *Grilled Chateaubriand*

1 to 1 ½ pound Chateaubriand (a thick slice from the middle of the filet)
3-4 tablespoons melted butter or oil (for basting)
Salt and freshly ground black pepper
Béarnaise Sauce

**Béarnaise Sauce**
3 tablespoons wine vinegar
6 peppercorns
½ bay leaf
Dash of mace
1 slice of onion
2 egg yolks
½ cup butter
Salt and pepper
1 teaspoon meat glaze
1 teaspoon tarragon
1 teaspoon chopped parsley
Pinch of chopped chives or a little grated onion

Put the vinegar, peppercorns, bay leaf, mace and slice of onion into a pan. Boil until reduced to 1 tablespoon. Set aside.

Place the yolks in a small bowl with ½ tablespoon butter and a pinch of salt and beat until thick. Strain in vinegar, set bowl on a pan of boiling water, turn off heat and stir until beginning to thicken.

Add remaining softened butter in small pieces, beating well after each addition. Add meat glaze, herbs and chives or onion and season with pepper. Finished sauce should be the consistency of whipped cream.

Brush the Chateaubriand with melted butter or oil. Sprinkle it with pepper and grill it for 20-25 minutes. Brush it often with melted butter or oil during cooking and turn it 2-3 times so it browns evenly on all sides. Sprinkle it lightly with salt. Serve it with Bernaise Sauce.

Let the meat stand in a warm place for 10 minutes before carving to let the juices 'set'. Carve in diagonal 1-inch slices, giving each person some of the brown outsides and rare inside slices.

## Grilled Delmonico Steaks

½ cup olive oil
¼ cup Worcestershire sauce
6 tablespoons soy sauce
¼ cup minced garlic
½ medium onion, chopped
2 tablespoons salt
1 tablespoon pepper
1 tablespoon crushed dried rosemary
3 tablespoons steak seasoning
3 tablespoons steak sauce (e.g. A-1)
4 (10-ounce) Delmonico (rib-eye) steaks

Combine the olive oil, Worcestershire sauce, soy sauce, garlic, onion, salt, pepper, rosemary, steak seasoning, and steak sauce in the container of a food processor or blender. Process until well blended.

Prick steaks on both sides with a fork, and place in a shallow container with a lid. Pour marinade over steaks, cover, and refrigerate at least 3 hours, or overnight.

Preheat an outdoor grill for medium heat. Soaked wood chips may be added to the coals when ready for a smoky flavor, if you like.

Remove steaks from marinade, and discard the marinade. Lightly oil the grilling surface, and place steaks on the grill. Cover, and grill steaks for about 10 minutes on each side, or to your desired degree of doneness.

## Grilled Steaks Balsamico

2/3 cup balsamic vinaigrette
¼ cup fig preserves
4 (6 to 8 ounce) boneless beef chuck-eye steaks
1 teaspoon salt
1 teaspoon freshly ground pepper
1 (6.5 ounce) container buttery garlic-and-herb spreadable cheese

Process vinaigrette and preserves in a blender until smooth. Place steaks and vinaigrette mixture in a shallow dish or a large zip-top plastic freezer bag. Cover or seal, and chill at least 2 hours. Remove steaks from marinade, discarding marinade.

Grill, covered with grill lid, over medium-high heat (350-400 degrees) 5-7 minutes on each side or until desired degree of doneness. Remove to a serving platter, and sprinkle evenly with salt and pepper; keep warm.

Heat cheese in a small saucepan over low heat, stirring often, 2-4 minutes or until melted. Serve cheese sauce with steaks.

## Grilled Steak Bites with Bloody Mary Sauce

1 tablespoon extra-virgin olive oil, plus more for drizzling
1 small onion, finely chopped
½ cup vodka
2 tablespoons Worcestershire sauce
2 teaspoons hot pepper sauce
1 cup tomato sauce
1 rounded tablespoon prepared horseradish
Kosher salt and freshly ground black pepper
1 1/3 pounds beef sirloin cut into large bite-sized pieces, about
1-inch squares
Steak seasoning blend or coarse salt and black pepper
6 to 8-inch bamboo skewers

Heat a small saucepan over medium heat. Add oil and onions
and sauté 5 minutes. Add vodka and boil to reduce by half. Add
Worcestershire, hot sauce, tomato sauce and horseradish.

Stir to combine the dipping sauce and return the sauce to a simmer.
Add salt and pepper and adjust seasonings.

Heat grill over medium high heat. Coat meat bites lightly in oil.
Season with steak seasoning blend or salt and pepper, to taste. Grill
the meat about 2 minutes on each side.

Transfer dipping sauce to a small dish and place at the center of
a serving platter. Surround the dip with meat bites and set several
bamboo "stakes" or skewers alongside meat.

## *Grilled Veal Medallions with Artichoke and Nicoise Olive Relish*

2 pounds boneless veal top round, trimmed and cut into 12 thin medallions
1 garlic clove, crushed
3 thyme sprigs, leaves removed
1 tablespoon olive oil
Kosher salt and freshly ground black pepper
Artichoke and Nicoise Olive Relish

Place the veal medallions on a platter and rub with the garlic. Sprinkle with the thyme, drizzle with the olive oil, and massage them into the veal. Cover and let rest at room temperature for 30 minutes.

Prepare a hot grill. Rub the grill rack with an oiled paper towel.

Season the medallions with salt and pepper and grill until the edges begin to turn opaque, 2-3 minutes. Turn and cook until just done, about 2 minutes more. Transfer the veal to a rack set over a plate and let rest briefly.

Arrange the veal on four plates and spoon the relish over the top.

### Artichoke and Nicoise Olive Relish

1 large red onion, cut into ½-inch-thick slices
6 baby artichokes, trimmed, quartered, and blanched in boiling water until tender
¼ cup Nicoise olives (or Picholine or other good-quality olives), pitted and chopped
1 shallot, finely minced
2 tablespoons sherry vinegar
3 tablespoons red wine vinegar
½ cup olive oil
6 sprigs basil, leaves removed and torn
5 sprigs flat-leaf parsley, leaves removed and torn

4 sprigs mint, leaves removed and torn
Kosher salt and freshly ground black pepper to taste
Grated zest of ½ lemon

Prepare a hot grill. Grill the onion slices, turning once, until charred on both sides, about 4 minutes per side. Allow them to cool, then cut into ¼-inch cubes.

In a bowl, combine the onions, artichokes, olives, shallot, vinegars, olive oil, and herbs and toss well to combine. Add the salt and pepper, along with the lemon zest. Taste and adjust the seasoning.

## Lover's Beef Burgundy Filet

4 cups Burgundy wine
1 ½ cups canola oil
1 ½ cups soy sauce
2 cups oyster sauce
1 tablespoon garlic, minced
1 ½ teaspoons dried oregano

8 (6-ounce) filet mignon filets

½ cup butter, softened
1 teaspoon Burgundy wine
1 tablespoon minced shallots
1 tablespoon minced green onions
1 teaspoon ground white pepper

In a medium saucepan, mix together Burgundy wine, canola oil, soy sauce, oyster sauce, garlic and oregano. Bring to a boil, and then remove from heat. Place in the refrigerator 1 hour, or until chilled.

Place filet mignon filets in a 9x13-inch baking dish, and pour the chilled marinade over them. Cover tightly with foil, and refrigerate for a minimum of 5 hours.

In a medium bowl, cream butter and 1 teaspoon of Burgundy wine with a hand mixer. Mix in shallots, green onions and white pepper by hand; cover tightly, and refrigerate.

Preheat an outdoor grill for high heat, and lightly oil grate. Preheat oven to 200 degrees.

Grill marinated filets to desired doneness, turning once. Place filets in a clean 9x13-inch baking dish. Dollop with the Burgundy butter mixture, and place in the preheated oven for a minute, or until butter is melted.

## *Marinated London Broil*

1 (12 ounce) can cola soft drink
1 (10 ounce) can bottle teriyaki sauce
1 (2 ½ to 3 pound) London Broil

Combine cola and teriyaki sauce in a shallow dish or large zip-top plastic freezer bag; add London broil. Cover or seal, and chill 24 hours, turning occasionally.

Remove London broil from marinade, discarding marinade.

Grill, covered with grill lid, over medium heat (300-350 degrees) 12-15 minutes on each side or to desired degree of doneness. Let stand 10 minutes; cut diagonally into thin slices across the grain.

## Sirloin Burgers with Mushrooms, Swiss, and Balsamic Mayo

Extra virgin olive oil
3 tablespoons finely chopped yellow onion
1 1/3 pounds ground sirloin, 90% lean
1 tablespoon Worcestershire sauce
Steak seasoning blend
4 crusty rolls, split
12 baby Portobello or crimini mushrooms, thinly sliced
Coarse salt and freshly ground black pepper, to taste
4 slices Swiss cheese
3 tablespoons aged balsamic vinegar
½ cup mayonnaise or reduced-fat mayonnaise
Freshly ground coarse black pepper, to taste
4 leaves romaine lettuce
2 vine-ripe tomatoes, sliced
2 scallions, sliced

Preheat grill for burgers over medium-high heat. In a small nonstick skillet over moderate heat, sauté chopped onion in a drizzle of olive oil for 2-3 minutes. Set pan aside.

In a medium bowl, combine meat with Worcestershire sauce, steak seasoning blend or salt and pepper. Mix in sautéed onion and form into 4 large patties. Drizzle patties with a touch of olive oil. Quick toast your split rolls on the hot grill pan or skillet and set aside. Add burgers to the grill for 4-5 minutes on each side for medium to medium-well burgers.

Return small nonstick skillet to stove over medium-high heat. Add 1 tablespoon olive oil and sliced mushrooms. Season with salt and pepper, then sauté' until just tender, about 3-5 minutes. Remove from heat.

Pile mushrooms on top of burgers just before you are ready to take them off the grill. Fold each slice of Swiss cheese in half and rest on top of mushrooms. Place a loose tin foil tent over the burgers and turn heat off. Allow the cheese to melt down over the mushrooms and burgers, about 3 minutes.

Combine balsamic vinegar, mayonnaise and lots of coarsely ground or cracked black pepper in a small dish.

To assemble, place burgers topped with mushrooms and Swiss cheese on bun bottom. Slather tops of buns with balsamic, black pepper, mayo, and add romaine. Set burger tops in place and serve with sliced tomatoes, drizzled with oil, seasoned with salt and pepper and garnished with sliced scallions. Pile thick-cut onion rings and a dollop of dipping sauce alongside.

## *Sizzling Peaches and Steak*

4 slices, thick-sliced bacon, cut crosswise into thirds
4 6-ounce beef boneless flat iron, rib eye, or Delmonico steaks, cut
¾ to 1-inch thick
Salt and ground black pepper
Nonstick cooking spray
1 recipe Peach Steak Sauce (see recipe below)
2 fresh peaches, pitted and cut into eighths
4 slices Texas toast, toasted

In a large skillet cook bacon until crisp and brown. Remove from skillet. Drain on paper towels; set aside. Reserve 1 tablespoon drippings in skillet; set aside.

Lightly season steaks with salt and pepper. Lightly coat the grilling rack with nonstick cooking spray. Reduce heat to medium and cook, uncovered, for 8-15 minutes for medium rare (145 degrees) to medium (160 degrees) doneness, turning occasionally. Use ½ cup of the Peach Steak Sauce to brush on steaks during the last 5 minutes of cooking.

Meanwhile, in the large skillet heat the reserved 1 tablespoon of bacon drippings. Add peaches and cook over medium-high heat for about 3 minutes or until peaches are browned and heated through, stirring and turning peaches occasionally.

To serve, place a toast slice on each plate. Top with bacon, a steak, and the peaches. Pass remaining Peach Steak Sauce.

**Peach Steak Sauce**: In a food processor bowl or blender container place 2 medium peeled, pitted, and cut up fresh peaches. Cover and process until almost smooth. In a small saucepan combine pureed peaches, ¼ cup peach or apricot nectar, 2 tablespoons condensed beef consommé or condensed beef broth, 2 tablespoons balsamic vinegar, 1 tablespoon packed brown sugar, 1 tablespoon minced onion, and 1/4 teaspoon ground cinnamon. Bring to boiling; reduce heat. Simmer, uncovered, for 10 minutes or until sauce reaches desired consistency, stirring occasionally. Makes 1 cup.

## Smoked Prime Rib

1 lip-on Rib-Eye (9-12 pounds)
½ cup Balsamic Vinegar
1-2 tablespoons kosher salt
1 tablespoon dried chopped garlic
1 tablespoon coarse or cracked black pepper
1 tablespoon dried rosemary, crushed

Rub the roast all over with the balsamic vinegar and season with each of the seasonings to taste. Smoke at 230-250 degrees for about 4 hours or until it reaches an internal temperature of 140 degrees for medium rare, or longer if desired. Slice to order and enjoy.

## Smoked Baby Back Ribs

1 2-pound rack of baby rack ribs
3 teaspoons of rub
1 teaspoon of sugar
1 cup of barbecue sauce

Skin the membrane off of the back side of the rack of ribs. Sprinkle with your favorite rub and the sugar. Smoke at 250 degrees for three hours. After two hours, baste with barbecue sauce.

## *Tom's Grilled Tenderloin*

Whole Beef Tenderloin
½ cup Canadian Steak Seasoning

Trim the tenderloin. Shake the Canadian Steak Seasoning generously over the tenderloin. Spray with non-stick cooking spray. Grill
over medium high heat for twelve minutes or until meat reaches
desired doneness.

To serve this steak dish, slice the steak in thin strips and serve with
your favorite sauce.

## *Tropical Fiesta Steak*

¼ cup frozen orange juice concentrate, thawed
3 tablespoons cooking oil
2 tablespoons honey
1 tablespoon spicy brown or Dijon-style mustard
1 tablespoon sliced green onion
1 teaspoon snipped fresh mint or ¼ teaspoon dried mint, crushed
Several dashes bottled hot pepper sauce
1 ½ pounds boneless beef sirloin steak, cut 1 to 1 ½ -inches thick
½ cup chopped red sweet pepper
½ cup chopped red apple
½ cup chopped pear
½ cup chopped peeled peach
¼ cup chopped celery
2 tablespoons sliced green onion
2 teaspoons lemon juice
Romaine leaves (optional)

For marinade, stir together orange juice concentrate, cooking oil, honey, mustard, the 1 tablespoon sliced green onion, mint, and hot pepper sauce in a small mixing bowl. Set aside ¼ cup of the mixture for the relish; cover and chill until needed.

Place the steak in a plastic bag set in a shallow bowl. Pour the remaining marinade over meat. Seal the bag and turn to coat the meat with marinade. Marinate in the refrigerator for 12 to 24 hours, turning the bag occasionally.

For relish, combine reserved ¼ cup marinade, sweet pepper, apple, pear, peach, celery, the 2 tablespoons green onion, and lemon juice in a medium bowl. Cover and chill up to 24 hours.

Remove the steak from the plastic bag, reserving marinade. Grill steak on the rack of an uncovered grill over medium heat to desired doneness, turning once and brushing occasionally with marinade until the last 10 minutes of grilling. Allow 18-22 minutes for medium (160 degrees) doneness for 1-inch-thick steak, or 36-40 minutes for medium (160 degrees) doneness for a 1 ½ -inch-thick steak.

To serve; bias-slice steak into thin strips, arrange on romaine leaves, if desired. Top steak with fruit relish.

# CHICKEN

## *Chicken Casserole*

6 grilled chicken breasts
2 cans cream of mushroom soup
2 red onions
2 baking potatoes, cooked and diced
1 pack sliced mushrooms
Canola oil
2 cans spinach
2 cups crushed Ritz crackers
2 cups shredded Mozzarella cheese
Butter
1 cup of cooked Instant Rice

Spray a cast iron skillet with non-stick cooking spray. Chop up chicken breasts. Slice onions 1-inch thick and spray with non-stick cooking spray. Grill two minutes on each side.

Drain spinach and spread evenly in the bottom of the cast iron skillet. In a large bowl, mix chicken breasts, mushroom soup, mushrooms, cheese, rice, and diced onions and potatoes. Place in the skillet and top with crushed Ritz crackers.

Grill over medium heat for twenty-five minutes.

## *Crunchy Apple Salsa with Grilled Chicken*

**Salsa**
2 cups apples, halved, cored and chopped
¾ cup (1 large) Anaheim chile pepper, seeded and chopped
½ cup chopped onion
¼ cup lime juice
Salt and pepper to taste

**Marinade**
¼ cup dry white wine
¼ cup apple juice
½ teaspoon grated lime peel
½ teaspoon salt
Dash pepper
4 medium boneless, skinless chicken breasts

Combine salsa ingredients and mix well. Allow flavors to blend about thirty minutes. Serve over or alongside grilled chicken. Makes 3 cups salsa.

For grilled chicken, combine marinade ingredients, pour over chicken breasts. Marinate for 20-30 minutes. Drain and grill over medium heat coals, turning once, until chicken is done.

# Grilled Honey Lime Chicken Sandwiches

The juice of 1 lime
2 tablespoons honey
1 rounded teaspoon cumin
A handful cilantro, finely chopped
2 tablespoons extra-virgin olive oil, canola or corn oil
4 boneless skinless chicken breasts
1 teaspoon steak seasoning blend

## Toppings
Lettuce, sliced tomato, red onion and avocado
1 cup prepared salsa verde
4 crusty rolls, split

Combine first 5 ingredients in a small bowl to make dressing. Sprinkle chicken with seasoning blend or slat and pepper. Coat chicken in dressing and set aside for 10 minutes.

Grill chicken 6-7 minutes on each side.

Slice grilled chicken on an angle and pile on roll bottoms. Top with lettuce, tomato, red onion and sliced avocado. Spread salsa on roll tops. Serve with Mexican Chunk Vegetable Salad, and assorted tortilla chips.

## *Grilled Filipino Chicken*

1 can lemonade or lime-and lemonade
2 tablespoons gin
4 tablespoons tomato ketchup
2 teaspoons garlic salt
2 teaspoons Worcestershire sauce
4 lean chicken supremes or breast fillets
Salt and pepper

**To Serve**
Thread egg noodles
1 green chili, chopped finely
2 scallions, sliced

Combine the lemonade or lime-and-lemonade, gin, tomato ketchup, garlic salt, Worcestershire sauce, and seasoning in a large non-porous dish. Put the chicken supremes into the dish and make sure that the marinade covers them completely.

Leave to marinate in the refrigerator for 2 hours. Remove and leave covered at room temperature for 30 minutes.

Place the chicken over a medium heat on the grill and cook for 20 minutes. Turn the chicken once, halfway through the cooking time. Remove from the grill and leave to rest for 3 or 4 minutes before serving.

Serve with egg noodles, tossed with a little green chili and scallions.

## *Indian Charred Chicken*

4 chicken breasts, skinned and boned
2 tablespoons curry paste
1 tablespoon sunflower oil
1 tablespoon light muscovado sugar
1 teaspoon ground ginger
½ teaspoon ground cumin

**To Serve**
Naan bread
Green salad leaves

**Cucumber Raita**
¼ cucumber
2/3 cup low-fat plain yogurt
¼ teaspoon chili powder

Place the chicken breasts between 2 sheets of baking parchment or plastic wrap. Pound them with the flat side of a meat mallet or rolling pin to flatten them.

Mix together the curry paste, oil, sugar, ginger, and cumin in a small bowl. Spread the mixture over both sides of the chicken and set aside until required.

To make the raita, peel the cucumber and scoop out the seeds with a spoon. Grate the cucumber flesh, sprinkle with salt, place in a sieve, and leave to stand for 10 minutes. Rinse off the salt and squeeze out any moisture by pressing the cucumber with the base of a glass or back of a spoon.

Mix the cucumber with the yogurt and stir in the chili powder. Leave to chill until required.

Transfer the chicken to an oiled rack and barbecue over hot coals for 10 minutes, turning once.

Warm the naan bread at the side of the barbecue.

Serve the chicken with the naan bread and raita and accompanied with fresh green salad leaves.

## *Israeli Spice Chicken*

4 boneless, skinless chicken breasts
Extra-virgin olive oil
4 tablespoons Israeli Spice Rub

**Israeli Spice Rub**
1 ½ tablespoons sweet paprika
1 ½ tablespoons ground cumin
1 teaspoon dried oregano
1 teaspoon ground coriander
1 teaspoon crushed red pepper flakes
1½ teaspoon coarse Kosher salt
Pita or flat bread

Place chicken breast in a shallow dish. Drizzle with extra-virgin olive oil to barely coat the meat. Rub both sides of chicken breast liberally with spice blend. Let stand 10 minutes.

Preheat grill to medium-high. Grill chicken 6 or 7 minutes on each side or until juices run clear. Serve with warm pita bread.

## Mediterranean Chicken

4 tablespoons low-fat plain yogurt
3 tablespoons sun-dried tomato paste
1 tablespoon olive oil
¼ cup fresh basil leaves, lightly crushed
2 garlic cloves, chopped roughly
4 chicken quarters
Green salad, to serve

Combine the yogurt, tomato paste, olive oil, basil leaves, and garlic in a small bowl and stir well to mix.

Put the marinade into a bowl large enough to hold the chicken quarters in a single layer. Add the chicken quarters. Make sure that the chicken pieces are thoroughly coated in the marinade.

Leave to marinate in the refrigerator for 2 hours. Remove and leave covered at room temperature for 30 minutes

Place the chicken over a medium barbecue and cook for 30-40 minutes, turning frequently. Test for readiness by piercing the flesh at the thickest part-usually at the top of the drumstick. If the juices that run out are clear, it is cooked through.

Serve hot with a green salad. It is also delicious eaten cold

## *Molasses-Glazed Chicken Thighs*

¾ cup molasses
1/3 cup soy sauce
¼ cup olive oil
3 garlic cloves, minced
1 teaspoon pepper
12 skinned and boned chicken thighs

Combine first 6 ingredients in a shallow dish or large zip-top plastic freezer bag; add chicken thighs. Cover or seal, and chill 8 hours, turning occasionally.

Remove chicken from marinade, discarding marinade.

Grill chicken thighs, covered with grill lid, over medium heat (300-350 degrees) 5-6 minutes on each side or until done.

## *Peanut Sauced Chicken Satay Kabobs*

4 large boneless, skinless chicken breast halves (1 pound total)
¾ cup soy sauce
2 tablespoons cooking oil
2 tablespoons lemon juice
1 teaspoon curry powder
1 teaspoon toasted sesame oil
¼ teaspoon ground coriander
1 clove garlic, minced
4 to 5 tablespoons hot water
¼ cup peanut butter
½ teaspoon grated gingerroot
1/8 teaspoon crushed red pepper

Rinse chicken; pat dry. Cut chicken breasts lengthwise into 1-inch-wide strips. Place chicken strips in a plastic bag set in a deep bowl. For marinade, combine soy sauce, cooking oil, lemon juice, curry powder, sesame oil, coriander, and garlic; pour over chicken. Close bag. Marinate in refrigerator for 1 to 2 hours, turning occasionally.

Meanwhile, for peanut sauce, in a small bowl gradually stir hot water into peanut butter till smooth and of a sauce-like consistency. Stir in gingerroot and red pepper. Set sauce aside.

Drain chicken, reserving marinade. On 8 long metal skewers, loosely thread chicken strips accordion-style. Preheat gas grill. Adjust heat for direct cooking. Place kabobs on grill rack over medium heat. Cover and grill kabobs for 5-6 minutes or until the chicken is tender and no longer pink, brushing occasionally with reserved marinade and turning once halfway through.

Serve chicken strips with peanut sauce. Makes 4 servings.

Indirect Grilling: Preheat gas grill. Adjust heat for indirect cooking. Place kabobs on grill rack over medium heat. Cover and grill kabobs for 7-8 minutes or till chicken is tender and no longer pink, brushing occasionally with reserved marinade and turning once halfway through. Continue as directed above.

## Smoked Chicken

Three pound chicken
Rub
1 cup of barbecue sauce

Wash the chicken. Sprinkle with your favorite rub. Split the breast down the middle. Lay backbone down, so the juices gather in the cavity of the bird. Smoke at 250 degrees for three hours. After two hours, baste with barbecue sauce.

## Smoky Orange Barbecued Chicken Sandwiches

1 tablespoon olive or vegetable oil
1 small onion, chopped
2 chipotle peppers (smoky hot) in adobo sauce
½ cup ketchup
¼ cup orange juice concentrate
Zest of 1 orange, wedge the orange
1 cup chicken broth
4 boneless, skinless chicken breasts
Vegetable oil
Steak seasoning blend

**Toppings**
Romaine lettuce
Thinly sliced red onions
4 crusty rolls, split, toasted and buttered

Preheat grill over medium-high heat.

Heat a small saucepan over moderate heat. Add oil and sauté onion 3-5 minutes or until soft. Combine chipotle peppers in adobo, ketchup, orange juice concentrate, orange zest and chicken broth in a blender. Blend on high until sauce is smooth. Pour sauce into saucepan with the onion and heat to a bubble. Reduce heat to simmer.

Coat chicken lightly with a drizzle of oil and season with grill seasoning blend or salt and pepper. Grill 5-6 minutes on the first side, turn. Remove half of the barbecue sauce to a small bowl and baste chicken liberally with it. Turn chicken after 4 minutes, coat with sauce again and cook another 2-3 minutes.

To serve sandwiches, slice grilled chicken on an angle and fan out 1 breast on each bun bottom. Spoon remaining sauce from saucepan over the sliced chicken. Serve open faced with the lettuce and red onions setting on bun tops to the side. Garnish with orange wedges.

## *Split Barbecued Chicken*

3 pound 5 ounces chicken
Grated rind of one lemon
4 tablespoons lemon juice
2 sprigs rosemary
1 small red chili, chopped finely
2/3 cup olive oil

Split the chicken down the breast bone and open it out. Trim off excess fat, and remove the parson's nose, wings, and leg tips. Break the leg and wing joints to enable you to pound it flat. This ensures that it cooks evenly. Cover the split chicken with plastic wrap and pound it as flat as possible with a rolling pin.

Mix the lemon rind and juice, rosemary sprigs, chili, and olive oil together in a small bowl. Place the chicken in a large dish and pour over the marinade, turning the chicken to coat it evenly. Cover the dish and leave the chicken to marinate for at least 2 hours.

Cook the chicken over a hot grill for about 30 minutes, turning it regularly for the first 15 minutes and until the skin is golden and crisp. Then, let the bird cook cavity side up. To test if it is cooked, pierce one of the chicken thighs; the juices will run clear, not pink, when it is ready.

## Super Moist Grilled Chicken

Chickens, cut-up and washed
Salt and pepper to taste.
3 cups of your favorite BBQ Sauce

Place a burn proof pan on one side of your grill and fill the pan
with apple juice, beer or water. Do not heat that side of the grill.
Preheat the other side of the grill to medium high heat.

Salt and pepper the chicken to taste. Spray each piece with nonstick cooking spray. Place the meat on the direct heat side of the
grill and brown each piece of chicken.

Then, move all of the chicken to the side of the grill that has no
direct heat. Close the grill for one hour. During the last twenty
minutes, baste the birds with BBQ sauce

# PORK

## *Cajun Pork Burgers*

¾ pound Andouille sausage, removed from casing
1 pound ground pork
1 rib celery, finely chopped
½ green bell pepper, finely chopped
1 small white onion, finely chopped
3 cloves garlic, minced
4 sprigs fresh thyme, chopped (about 1 tablespoon) or 1 teaspoon dried thyme
1 teaspoon cayenne pepper sauce (several drops)
Coarse salt and freshly ground black pepper, to taste

**Special Sauce**
½ cup chili sauce
¼ cup mayo or reduced-fat mayonnaise
¼ cup prepared sweet red pepper relish

**Toppings**
Bibb lettuce or hearts of romaine
Sliced vine-ripe tomato

5 crusty rolls, split

Cut sausage into large chunks and place in a food processor. Grind sausage into crumbles, and combine in a bowl with pork, vegetables, thyme, hot sauce, and a little salt and pepper. Form mixture into patties and grill 7 minutes on each side on a grill preheated to medium high.

Mix chili sauce, mayo, and sweet relish in a small bowl. Serve burgers on crusty rolls with special sauce, lettuce and tomato.

## Grilled Sugarcane Ham with Spiced Apples and Pears

12 sugarcane swizzle sticks, each cut into about 3-inch pieces
1 hickory smoked ham, spiral sliced, 8 to 10 pounds (no bone,
water added, cooked)
1 cup firmly packed light brown sugar
1 cup pure cane syrup
½ cup dark molasses
½ cup dark corn syrup
1/8 teaspoon freshly grated nutmeg
¼ teaspoon ground cloves
1/8 teaspoon ground allspice
½ teaspoon ground cinnamon
1 teaspoon dry mustard
¼ cup water
1 ½ pounds (about 4) Granny Smith apples
1 ½ pounds (about 4) Bartlett pears
2 dozen medium buttermilk biscuits

Preheat the grill to medium heat.

Insert the sugarcane sticks into the ham at 3 to 4-inch intervals. Tie
the ham, using kitchen twine, horizontally and vertically to keep
it together, like wrapping a gift. Place on a wire rack in the baking
pan.

In a mixing bowl, combine all of the ingredients together except
for the mustard and water. Mix well. In a small bowl, dissolve the
mustard in the water, then add to the spice mixture. Blend well.
Brush the entire ham with the glaze, coating it evenly.

Wash, core, and halve the fruit. Place all around the ham. Baste the
ham a second time and baste the fruit with the glaze. Cook using
the indirect grilling method. After the entire grill is preheated, turn
the heat off on one side of the grill and place the baking pan on the
side of the grill with no direct heat.

Grill for 45 minutes. Baste the ham and fruit again. Grill another 45 minutes.
Remove the ham from the grill and let it rest for 5 minutes.
Remove and discard the string and swizzle sticks.

Serve the apples and pears on a platter with the ham. Serve everything warm or at room temperature.

# Grilled Molasses Glazed Pork with Sweet Potatoes

4 cloves garlic, peeled
½ teaspoon salt
3 ½ tablespoons molasses
3 ½ tablespoons fresh lime juice
2 teaspoons ground cumin
Freshly ground black pepper to taste
2 ¾-pound pork tenderloins, trimmed of fat
¾ cup reduced-sodium chicken broth
1 tablespoon olive oil
2 medium red onions, cut into 8 wedges each
3 medium sweet potatoes, peeled, halved lengthwise and cut into
1-inch slices
1 10 ounce package frozen whole okra
1 tablespoon chopped fresh thyme or 1 teaspoon dried thyme leaves

With the side of a chef's knife, mash garlic and salt into a paste.
Transfer to a large shallow dish. Stir in 2 tablespoons molasses, 2
tablespoons lime juice, cumin and pepper to taste. Add pork and
coat well. Cover and marinate in the refrigerator, turning occasionally, for at least 1 hour or overnight.

Preheat the grill to medium high heat.

In a 10 x 14-inch roasting pan, whisk chicken broth, remaining 1 ½
tablespoons molasses, remaining 1 ½ tablespoon lime juice and oil.
Add onions, sweet potatoes, okra and thyme; season with salt and
pepper to taste and toss well. Cover tightly with foil.
Grill the vegetables for 25 to 30 minutes, or until sweet potatoes
begin to soften.

Push vegetables to sides of pan. Place pork in center and pour any
remaining marinade over it. Roast, uncovered, until just a trace
of pink remains in the center and an instant-read thermometer
inserted in the thickest part registers 155 degrees, 30 to 35 minutes.
Transfer pork to a cutting board and let rest for 5 minutes

## Margarita Pork Tenderloin

3 garlic cloves, minced
1 green onion, minced
½ Jalapeno pepper, minced
3 tablespoons chopped fresh cilantro
2 tablespoons fresh lime juice
1 ½ tablespoons tequila
1 tablespoon fresh orange juice
1 teaspoon salt
1 teaspoon ground cumin
½ teaspoon chili powder
2 (1-pound) pork tenderloins

Combine first 10 ingredients in a shallow dish or large zip-top plastic freezer bag. Cut pork diagonally into 1-inch-thick slices, and add to tequila mixture. Cover or seal and chill 1 hour, turning occasionally.

Remove pork from marinade, discarding marinade.

Grill, covered with grill lid, over high heat (400 to 500 degrees) 3-4 minutes on each side or until done.

## Mustard Rubbed Chops

Bone-in pork chops, 1 ¼ inches thick
½ teaspoon garlic powder
2 teaspoons black pepper
1 tablespoon dry mustard
1 ½ teaspoons salt
1 ½ teaspoons paprika
1 ½ teaspoons dried, crushed basil

In a small bowl, stir together the garlic powder, black pepper, mustard, salt, paprika, and basil.

Sprinkle the rub over both sides of each chop. Place in a ziplock bag and refrigerate for two hours. Grill over medium heat for twenty-five minutes or until juices run clear.

## *Pork Chops Pockets*

4 ¾-inch thick pork chops, bone in
2 onions, slivered
4 medium potatoes, cut into thick fries
Bag of baby carrots

### Pork Chop Pocket Rub
2 tablespoons black pepper
2 tablespoons thyme
2 tablespoons white pepper
2 tablespoons onion powder
2 tablespoons seasoning salt
2 tablespoons cayenne pepper
1 tablespoon basil
1 tablespoon parsley

Take two sheets of heavy-duty aluminum foil for each pocket.
Spray the foil sheets with nonstick cooking spray.

Combine all of the rub ingredients and mix together. Sprinkle the
pork chops with rub and place one pork chop in each pocket. Top
each pork chop with ¼ of the onion slivers, ¼ of the fries and
seven baby carrots.

Seal the foil sheets, but leave room for the steam to rise. Grill over
medium heat for thirty-five minutes.

## Smoked Pork Tenderloin

7 pound pork tenderloin
½ cup of rub
1 cup of barbecue sauce

Sprinkle with your favorite rub. Smoke at 250 degrees for three hours. After two hours, baste with barbecue sauce.

## *Tangy Pork Fillet*

14 ounce lean pork fillet
3 tablespoons orange marmalade
Grated rind and juice of 1 orange
1 tablespoon white wine vinegar
Dash or Tabasco sauce
Salt and pepper

### Sauce
1 tablespoon olive oil
1 small onion, chopped
1 small green bell pepper, deseeded and thinly sliced
1 tablespoon cornstarch
2/3 cup orange juice

Place a large piece of double thickness foil in a shallow dish. Put the pork fillet in the center of the foil, and season.

Heat the marmalade, orange rind and juice, vinegar, and Tabasco sauce in a small pan, stirring until the marmalade melts and the ingredients combine. Pour the mixture over the pork and wrap the meat in foil, making sure that the parcel is well sealed so that the juices cannot run out. Place over a medium heat grill for about 25 minutes, turning the parcel occasionally.

For the sauce, heat the oil and cook the onion for 2-3 minutes. Add the bell pepper and cook for 3-4 minutes. Remove the pork from the foil and place on to the rack. Pour the juices into the pan with the sauce.

Grill the pork for a further 10-20 minutes, turning, until cooked through and golden on the outside.

In a small bowl, mix the cornstarch with a little orange juice to form a paste. Add to the sauce with the remaining cooking juices. Cook, stirring, until the sauce thickens. Slice the pork, spoon over the sauce, and serve with rice and tossed salad leaves.

## *Thai Pork Chops with Caramelized Onions*

3 tablespoons brown sugar
3 tablespoons peanut butter
2 tablespoons soy sauce
2 teaspoons grated fresh ginger
1 garlic clove, minced
¼ to ½ teaspoon dried crushed red pepper
1 large sweet onion, sliced
1/3 cup orange juice
4 (1-inch-thick) boneless pork chops
½ teaspoon salt

Cook first 6 ingredients in a small saucepan over medium-high heat, stirring constantly, 1-2 minutes or until thoroughly heated. Add sliced onion, and sauté 15 minutes or until onion is caramelized. Remove and reserve onion with a slotted spoon, reserving liquid.

Stir orange juice into reserved liquid in pan. Brush mixture evenly over pork chops, and sprinkle evenly with salt.

Grill pork, covered with grill lid, over medium-high heat 4-5 minutes on each side or until done. Baste with orange juice mixture when you turn the meat. Remove to a serving platter; top with caramelized onion.

# SEAFOOD

## *Coaled and Tinned Trout*

1 whole (10-ounce) trout, pan-dressed
2 tablespoons butter
2 tablespoons lemon juice
1 teaspoon honey
½ teaspoon ground cayenne pepper
½ teaspoon lemon pepper

Place trout on center of a sheet of foil. Rub the inners of the trout with the butter. Drizzle lemon juice and honey all over the trout, inside and out. Sprinkle chile pepper inside as well. Sprinkle a little water (to keep it moist).

Place other sheet of foil on top, roll sides tight. Place package directly on top of hot coals and pile 5-10 coals on top of package. Cook for 8-12 minutes, or until you can hear it sizzling. Cool, cut open foil, and then enjoy.

## Crab Mousse

1 (10 to12-ounce) can cream of mushroom soup
1 (8-ounce) package cream cheese
1 envelope unflavored gelatin, softened in ¼ cup water
8 ounces lump crabmeat
1 cup finely chopped celery
¼ cup chopped green onion
1 tablespoon lemon juice
1 teaspoon Worcestershire sauce
¼ teaspoon seasoned salt

Grease a 3-cup seafood mold. Combine the soup, cream cheese, and softened gelatin in a saucepan and heat on the grill until hot and bubbly, about 5 minutes. Stir well to make sure that the gelatin is completely dissolved and that there are no lumps.

Add the crabmeat, celery, green onions, lemon juice, Worcestershire sauce, and seasoned salt. Stir gently but thoroughly. Spoon the mixture into the prepared mold and smooth the top with a spatula or knife. Cover with plastic wrap. Transfer to the refrigerator and chill until firm, about 3 to 6 hours.

When ready to serve, remove the plastic wrap and loosen the edges of the mousse by running a knife around the sides. Invert onto a serving dish. The mousse will slip out in a few minutes. Serve with crackers.

## Fish Pockets

4 Fish Filets
2 lemons, quartered
2 onions, cut in half and slivered
Salt and pepper to taste

Take two sheets of heavy-duty aluminum foil for each filet. Spray the foil sheets with nonstick cooking spray. Salt and pepper the filets. Place filets on the aluminum foil. Cover each filet with ¼ of the onion slivers.

Take two lemon quarters and squeeze the juice over the fish. Place the lemon quarters on top of the onions. Seal the foil sheets, but leave room for the steam to rise.

Grill over medium heat for thirty minutes.

## Gorgonzola Oysters

10 oysters
3 ounces gorgonzola cheese
½ garlic clove, chopped
¼ cup bread crumbs
2 tablespoons butter, softened

Preheat the oven to 350 degrees. Open the oysters and discard
their liquid. In a small bowl, combine the gorgonzola, garlic, bread
crumbs, and butter. Mix well. Place the oysters on a baking sheet.
Pour the gorgonzola mixture over them. Bake for 10 minutes.

## Grilled Red Snapper with Avocado Sauce

*It's the shape of the avocado, particularly when cut open, that gave this fruit its aphrodisiac reputation. Combine the creamy sauce with a bit of a kick delivered by horseradish with the delicate but strong-flavored snapper and you've got a winner for your lover.*

2 red snapper fillets
½ cup red wine
2 tablespoons melted butter, divided
1 teaspoon paprika
2 tablespoons finely chopped onion
1 tablespoon flour
¼ teaspoon seasoned salt
½ cup water
¼ cup sour cream
1 tablespoon horseradish
1 small ripe avocado, peeled and diced
1 lemon, quartered
1 tablespoon minced fresh parsley

Combine the fillets and wine in a shallow dish. Marinate at least 1 hour, drain. Brush 1 tablespoon butter on both sides of the filets. Sprinkle with paprika and grill 4-5 minutes or until done.

While grilling, sauté the onions in the remaining butter in a medium skillet until tender. Whisk in the flour and salt. Add water slowly. Cook for one minute, stirring constantly.

Remove the skillet from the heat. Stir in the sour cream, horse-radish and avocado. Return skillet to low heat and warm until heated through. Spoon sauce over the fillets and sprinkle with lemon juice and parsley.

## *Grilled Halibut Sandwiches*

1 ¼ to 1 ½ pounds fresh halibut, cut into 4 servings
Vegetable or olive oil, for drizzling
2 teaspoons Old Bay Seasoning
Salt and freshly ground black pepper, to taste
2 tablespoons butter, melted
The juice of ½ lemon

1 large ripe tomato, sliced
4 leaves green leaf or Boston lettuce
4 crusty rolls, split

**Zesty Tartar Sauce**
1 cup mayonnaise or reduced-fat mayonnaise
2 tablespoons sweet pickle relish
1 dill or half-sour pickle, finely chopped
2 tablespoons onion finely chopped
2 tablespoons fresh dill chopped
10 blades fresh chives, chopped or 2 thin scallions thinly sliced
The juice of ½ lemon
A few drops cayenne pepper sauce

Preheat the grill over medium-high heat. Drizzle halibut with oil, season with Old Bay, salt and pepper, and grill 4 or 5 minutes on each side.

Place melted butter in a small dish and add juice of ½ lemon.

Combine all ingredients for the tartar sauce in a small bowl: mayonnaise, sweet relish, chopped dill or half-sour pickle, onion, dill, chives, lemon, and pepper sauce. Stir to combine.

Lightly toast buns on grill when you remove fish from heat.

To assemble, brush bun bottoms and fish with lemon butter. Top fish with tomato and lettuce and slather the bun tops with tartar sauce, then serve.

# Parmesan Breaded Scallops

20 large sea scallops
2 tablespoons extra virgin olive oil

**For the Coating**
½ cup bread crumbs
¼ cup grated Parmesan Cheese
½ teaspoon salt
½ teaspoon black pepper

**For the Garnish**
½ cup parsley leaves
1 teaspoon extra virgin olive oil
1 teaspoon lemon juice

Combine the coating ingredients on a plate and mix with your fingers. Wash scallops and pat dry with a paper towel. Place in a bowl. Mix in the oil. Dip the scallops in the coating, turning to coat evenly. Gently press the crumbs into the scallops. Place the scallops in a single layer on a clean plate and cover with plastic wrap. Refrigerate for 1 hour to set the crumbs.

Finely chop the garnish ingredients, mix together and set aside. Spray the scallops with oil and place on the grill two inches apart, over high heat for three minutes. Turn and cook another three minutes. Remove from the grill and sprinkle with the garnish.

## *Peppered Tuna With Mushroom Sauce*

3 tablespoons butter
1 cup sliced fresh mushrooms
¾ cup plum sauce
¼ cup lite soy sauce
1 teaspoon dried ground ginger
2 tablespoons vegetable oil
6 (6 oz.) Tuna steaks (about 1 ½ -inches thick)
1 tablespoon freshly ground multicolored peppercorns*

Melt butter in a large skillet over medium-high heat until lightly browned. Add mushrooms and sauté 4-7 minutes or until lightly browned and tender. Stir in plum sauce, soy sauce, and ginger. Bring to a boil, reduce heat, and simmer, stirring often, 3-4 minutes. Keep warm.

Sprinkle tuna evenly with pepper and spray with nonstick cooking spray. Preheat your grill to medium high heat and grill the tuna 4 minutes on each side (rare) or to desired degree of doneness. Serve with warm sauce.

## Seared Tuna with Celery and Butter Pea Salad

1½ teaspoons peppercorns
1 teaspoon fennel seeds
1 8-ounce piece of center-cut tuna loin, about 3x3x4 inches
2 teaspoons olive oil
Kosher salt

**For the Salad**
2 celery stalks, cut lengthwise in half and sliced ¼-inch thick
1 cup canned chickpeas
1 red bell pepper, roasted, peeled, and seeded,
and cut into ½-inch dice
3 large button mushrooms, trimmed, cleaned,
and cut into julienne strips
1 shallot, finely minced
2 tablespoons extra virgin olive oil
1½ teaspoons red wine vinegar
Grated zest and juice of 1 lemon
Freshly ground black pepper

Toast the peppercorns and fennel seeds in a small skillet over
medium heat just until fragrant, about 3 minutes. Transfer to a
mortar and crush with the pestle, or crush under a heavy skillet.
Spread the crushed peppercorns and fennel seeds on a small plate.

Roll the tuna "brick" in the spices and press with the heel of
your hand so they adhere. Season the tuna with kosher salt and
drizzle with olive oil. Grill the tuna on all sides over high heat, 3-4
minutes total; it will be very rare inside. Transfer the tuna to a rack
set over a plate to rest.

To prepare the salad, combine the celery, peas, roasted pepper,
shallot, and lemon zest in a medium bowl and season with salt and
pepper. Toss with the extra virgin olive oil, vinegar, and lemon
juice.

Slice the tuna crosswise into 1/8 to ¼-inch thick slices and arrange like a sunburst in a circle on each of four serving plates. Place the salad in the center and drizzle the tuna with any remaining dressing from the bowl.

## Shrimp Cocktail with Rach's Quick Remoulade

30 large to jumbo raw shrimp, peeled and de-veined
Montreal Seasoning, to taste

**Remoulade**
1 ½ cups mayonnaise
½ cup Creole mustard
The juice of 1 lemon
2 teaspoons cayenne pepper sauce
1 rib celery, finely chopped
2 scallions, thinly sliced

Sprinkle shrimp with Montreal Steak Seasoning and spray nonstick cooking spray. Place in oiled grilling wok and grill over medium heat for about five minutes, stirring often.

Remove from grill and serve with Remoulade.

# TURKEY

## *Greek Turkey Burgers*

1 pound ground turkey
1/3 cup breadcrumbs
1 egg white, beaten
1 tablespoon milk
¼ cup Italian salad dressing
1 tablespoon white wine vinegar
2 teaspoons olive oil
2 tablespoons Italian salad dressing
1 cup finely chopped tomato
¼ cup finely chopped cucumber
¼ cup finely chopped black olives
¼ cup crumbled feta cheese

Combine eggs white, breadcrumbs and ¼ cup salad dressing in a bowl. Add ground turkey and mix well. Make into four patties. Grill patties over medium heat for sixteen minutes, turning once.

Combine vinegar, olive oil, remaining salad dressing, cucumber, tomatoes, and olives.

Serve burgers on grilled pita rounds. Top with tomato-olive topping and sprinkle with feta cheese.

## Grilled Turkey Breast in Plum Sauce

1 skinless turkey breast (3 to 3 ½ pounds)
1 cup apricot nectar
6 large plums, peeled and diced
2 jalapeno peppers, minced with the seeds removed
¼ cup olive oil
¼ cup green onions, minced
¼ cup fresh cilantro, minced
3 tablespoons soy sauce
3 tablespoons brown sugar
½ teaspoon black pepper

Combine apricot nectar, olive oil, soy sauce, and black pepper. Place turkey breast in a resealable bag. Cover with all but ¾ cup of marinade mixture. Turn to coat. Place both the bag and the ¾ cup of marinade (covered) in the refrigerator and let sit overnight.

Preheat grill and prepare for indirect grilling. Remove turkey breast from marinade and discard the marinade. Place turkey breast on grill and cook indirectly for 1 ½ to 2 hours. Breast will be done when it reaches an internal temperature of 170 degrees. Baste occasionally with the ¾ cup of marinade you saved.

Meanwhile combine the plums with peppers, onions, cilantro and brown sugar. Serve with turkey breast.

## Grilled Turkey Tenderloin with Stuffing

¼ cup lemon juice
3 tablespoons olive oil
½ teaspoon salt
¼ teaspoon pepper
½ teaspoon dried thyme leaves
½ teaspoon dried tarragon leaves
3 (12 ounce) turkey breast tenderloins
8-serving-size turkey or chicken stuffing mix

Mix lemon juice, oil, salt, pepper, thyme, and tarragon in a glass baking dish. Add turkey tenderloins and turn to coat. Cover with plastic wrap and refrigerate at least 1 hour but not longer than 24 hours.

Brush grill rack with vegetable oil and heat grill. Grease a 9-inch square aluminum pan and set aside. Remove turkey tenderloins from marinade and place directly on grill. Cover grill and cook turkey 4-5 inches from medium coals for 15 minutes. Meanwhile, in large bowl stir stuffing mix together with amount of water called for on package. Spoon into prepared aluminum pan and cover with foil.

Add pan with stuffing to grill rack. Brush turkey with marinade and turn. Discard remaining marinade. Cover and grill 10-15 minutes longer or until center is no longer pink or internal temperature reaches 180 degrees and stuffing is hot and tender. Let turkey and stuffing stand for 10 minutes before serving. Cut tenderloins into 1-inch pieces and serve with stuffing.

## Smoked Tom Turkey

12 pound turkey, cleaned and washed
1 cup Mr. BBQ's Magic Meat Marinade
Garlic salt and black pepper to taste

Prepare the grill for indirect cooking. Place a pan of apple juice directly under the grate where the turkey will cook. Turn the heat on the opposite side of the grill and preheat the grill to 250 degrees.

Inject turkey, all over, with Mr. BBQ's Magic Meat Marinade. Salt and pepper the bird to taste. Spray the bird with nonstick cooking spray.

Place the turkey on the grill and cook at 250 degrees for four hours, or until the bird reaches an internal temperature of 170 degrees.

## Smoked Turkey on the Grill

1 turkey, 12 to 14 pounds
2 quarts apple juice
1 pound brown sugar
1 cup kosher salt
3 oranges, quartered
4 ounces fresh ginger, thinly sliced
15 whole cloves
6 bay leaves
6 large cloves garlic, crushed
Cooking string for trussing turkey
Roasting rack
Heavy-gauge foil pan
Hickory chips

Combine apple juice, brown sugar and salt in a large saucepan. Bring to a boil and continue heating until the sugar and salt have dissolved. Skim off any foam that forms on the top and let cool. In a large (5 gallon or more) stock pot or similar container combine apple juice mixture, 3 quarts of water, oranges, ginger, cloves, bay leaves and garlic.

Wash turkey. Remove any fatty deposited you might find and everything from the body cavity. Place turkey in brine mixture and refrigerate for 24 hours. Make sure that the turkey remains completely submerged. Place hickory chips in water and prepare grill for indirect grilling on a medium heat.

Remove turkey from brine and pat dry with paper towels. Tie legs together with string and lightly brush turkey with vegetable oil. Place turkey on roasting rack inside a foil pan. Place on grill away from direct heat. After 30-40 minutes you will need to wrap the wings in foil to keep them from burning. Brush with vegetable oil periodically. If the breasts start to get too brown, cover with foil. The smoked turkey is done when the internal temperature reaches about 175 degrees in the thigh or about 165 in the breast.

You should expect it to take about 12-14 minutes per pound. When done remove from grill and let rest for about 15 minutes before you start carving.

# WILD GAME

## *Grilled Wild Boar Chops with Honey-Mustard Apricot Glaze*

8 wild Boar chops
Olive oil

**Mustard Apricot Glaze**
¼ pound dried apricots
1 ½ cups water
2 tablespoons unsalted butter
¼ cup finely minced shallots
2/3 cup white wine vinegar
¼ cup Dijon mustard
½ cup honey
1 teaspoon salt
1/3 teaspoon freshly ground white pepper

In a heavy saucepan, combine the apricots and water. Bring to a boil, reduce heat, and simmer uncovered for 12-15 minutes or until the apricots are tender and the liquid is reduced by half. In a separate sauté pan, melt the butter and sauté the shallots until softened but not brown. Transfer the apricot mixture and the shallots to a food processor along with the vinegar, mustard, honey, salt, and white pepper and puree until smooth. Return the mixture to the sauce pan and bring to a simmer. Simmer uncovered 8-10 minutes or until thickened. (Glaze can be cooked and stored in the refrigerator for up to 3 weeks).

Marinate the boar chops in a cup of the glaze for several hours or overnight in the refrigerator.

Heat grill on medium heat. Lift chops from marinade and drain briefly, reserving marinade. Place chops on a lightly greased grill.

Cook, brushing occasionally with marinade and turning once, until meat near bone is no longer pink, about 4-5 minutes per side.

## Grilled Rosemary Quail

Quail
¼ cup olive oil
Teaspoon fresh minced rosemary
3 teaspoons red wine vinegar
Salt and pepper to taste

Mix the oil, salt, pepper, vinegar, and rosemary. Place the quail in a ziplock bag and cover with the marinade. Seal the bag and refrigerate for two hours.

Heat the grill to medium high heat. Place the quail breast side down. Grill three minutes. Turn and grill two additional minutes.

## *Venison Kabobs*

Venison chunks from the backstrap or ham
2 pounds of bacon slices
1 cup Zesty Italian Dressing
1 cup Moore's Marinade
2 green bell peppers
2 medium onions
10 mushrooms

Trim meat and cut into bite sized pieces. Combine the Moore's Marinade and Italian Salad Dressing. Place meat in a ziplock bag and pour marinade mixture over the meat. Seal the ziplock bag and refrigerate for thirty six hours.

Wrap each piece of meat in bacon. Cut vegetables into chucks. Alternate meat and vegetables on a kabob stick. Grill over medium heat until the bacon is cooked.

# MARINADES, SAUCES AND RUBS

—ᴍ—

## MARINADES

### Tips for Using Marinades

- Marinating not only adds flavor, it helps keep meat and poultry moist.
- Chicken absorbs flavors quickly and does not require lengthy marinating. Even a brief half hour while the grill is heating is sufficient. Or, you can marinate it several hours or overnight.
- Always marinate meat and poultry in the refrigerator. Use a non-reactive container — glass, ceramic, or non-metallic bowl or a re-sealable plastic bag. Turn the meat or poultry several times to expose all sides to the marinade.
- Never reuse marinade. If some of the marinade is desired for basting during cooking, it is best to set aside a portion before uncooked meat or poultry is added to the remainder.
- If a marinade is used as the base for a sauce, bring it to a boil before applying it to the meat or poultry.

Here are some suggested base marinades. These suggestions make enough for approximately 4 servings of meat or poultry:

- ¼ cup light soy sauce, 1 tablespoon sesame oil, 1 garlic clove (minced), 1 teaspoon ginger and ½ teaspoon minced parsley leaves.
- 1/3 cup plain yogurt, 2 tablespoons minced green onion, 2 tablespoons chopped toasted almonds, ½ teaspoon coriander and ½ teaspoon dried crushed red pepper flakes.

- 2 tablespoons prepared mustard, ¼ cup soy sauce, 4 teaspoons honey, 1 tablespoon lemon juice and ¼ teaspoon ground ginger.
- ¼ cup olive oil, 1 tablespoon lemon juice, ½ teaspoon rosemary and ½ teaspoon thyme.

## *Beef Marinade*

1 ½ cups vegetable oil
¾ cup soy sauce
½ cup white wine vinegar
1/3 cup lemon juice
¼ cup Worcestershire sauce
2 tablespoons ground dry mustard
2 ¼ teaspoons salt
1 tablespoon ground black pepper
1 ½ tablespoons chopped fresh parsley
2 tablespoons ground cloves

In a quart jar, combine oil, soy sauce, vinegar, lemon juice and Worcestershire sauce. Season with mustard, salt, pepper, parsley and ground cloves. Shake well until it is mixed.

Put meat in a large bowl. Pour marinade over meat and let stand covered 3 days in refrigerator, basting every day.

## *Fajita Marinade*

¼ cup lime juice
1/3 cup water
2 tablespoons olive oil
4 cloves garlic, crushed
2 teaspoons soy sauce
1 teaspoon salt
½ teaspoon liquid smoke flavoring
½ teaspoon cayenne pepper
½ teaspoon ground black pepper

In a large re-sealable plastic bag, mix together the lime juice, water, olive oil, garlic, soy sauce, salt, and liquid smoke flavoring. Stir in cayenne and black pepper.

Place desired meat in the marinade, and refrigerate at least 2 hours, or overnight. Cook as desired.

## Korean BBQ Chicken Marinade

1 cup white sugar
1 cup soy sauce
1 cup water
1 teaspoon onion powder
1 teaspoon ground ginger
1 tablespoon lemon juice (optional)
4 teaspoons hot chile paste (optional)

In a medium saucepan over high heat, whisk together the sugar, soy sauce, water, onion powder, and ground ginger. Bring to a boil. Reduce heat to low, and simmer 5 minutes. Remove the mixture from heat, cool, and whisk in lemon juice and hot chile paste. Place chicken in the mixture. Cover, and marinate in the refrigerator at least 4 hours before preparing chicken as desired.

## Mr. BBQ's Magic Meat Marinade

1/3 cup olive oil
1/3 cup balsamic vinegar
1/3 cup soy sauce
1/3 cup Worcestershire sauce

Mix all four ingredients. Place in an airtight storage container, refrigerate and store for up to four weeks.

## *Teriyaki Marinade*

1/3 cup grated fresh ginger
1/3 cup minced garlic
1 ½ cups dry vermouth, divided
5 cups soy sauce
1 cup honey, or as needed
1 ¾ cups oyster sauce

In a large saucepan, combine ginger, garlic, and 1 cup vermouth. Bring to a boil over medium heat, and cook until ginger and garlic are tender.

Stir in remaining vermouth, soy sauce, honey, and oyster sauce. Bring to a low boil, and reduce heat to low. Simmer for 15 minutes to 1 hour; longer is better, but 15 minutes will do in a pinch. Watch carefully to be sure that the mixture does not foam and boil over.

Remove marinade from heat, and taste. The sauce should be sweet, not salty. If necessary, add up to 1 more cup of honey. Cool to room temperature. Marinade can be refrigerated for 4 to 5 days.

# SAUCES

## *Alabama White Barbecue Sauce*

1 cup mayonnaise
1 cup cider vinegar
1 tablespoon lemon juice
1 ½ tablespoons black pepper
½ teaspoon salt
¼ teaspoon cayenne

Mix ingredients together and refrigerate for at least 8 hours before using. Brush lightly over chicken, turkey or pork during the last few minutes of grilling. This barbecue sauce is also great as a dipping sauce so set some aside before you start grilling to serve on the table

## *Apple City Barbecue Sauce*

1 cup ketchup
2/3 cup seasoned rice vinegar
½ cup apple juice or cider
¼ cup apple cider vinegar
½ cup packed brown sugar
¼ cup soy sauce or Worcestershire sauce
2 teaspoons prepared yellow mustard
¾ teaspoon garlic powder
¼ teaspoon ground white pepper
¼ teaspoon cayenne
1/3 cup bacon bits, ground in a spice grinder
1/3 cup peeled and grated apple
1/3 cup grated onion
2 teaspoons grated green bell pepper

Combine the ketchup, rice wine vinegar, apple juice or cider, cider vinegar, brown sugar, soy sauce or Worcestershire sauce, mustard, garlic powder, white pepper, cayenne, and bacon bits in a large saucepan. Bring to a boil over medium-high heat.

Stir in the apple, onion, and bell pepper. Reduce the heat and simmer, uncovered, 10 to 15 minutes or until it thickens slightly. Stir it often. Allow to cool, then pour into sterilized glass bottles. A glass jar that used to contain mayonnaise or juice works well. Refrigerate for up to 2 weeks.

VARIATION: To make this sauce a little hotter, add more cayenne pepper to taste, approximately another ¼ to ½ teaspoon. Be careful; a little cayenne goes a long way.

## Coca Cola Sauce

½ cup cola
½ cup ketchup
2 tablespoons Worcestershire sauce
½ teaspoon instant onion flakes
½ teaspoon instant minced garlic
1 ½ teaspoons steak sauce (such as A-1)
½ teaspoon liquid smoke
¼ teaspoon black pepper

Mix all of the ingredients together and heat over low heat for fifteen minutes, stirring often.

## *Honey Barbecue Sauce*

3 cups chopped onion
¼ cup honey
1 tablespoon garlic, chopped
2 tablespoons lemon juice
1 cup sweet pepper, chopped
1 tablespoon salt
½ cup parsley, dried
3 tablespoons Worcestershire sauce
1 cup dry white wine
3 tablespoons vinegar
1 tablespoon liquid smoke
2 cups ketchup
½ tablespoon Louisiana hot sauce
Place all ingredients in a large saucepan. Bring to a boil. Simmer, covered, over very low heat for 2 to 3 hours.

## *Jack Daniels Barbecue Sauce*

Jack Daniels, about ½ to ¾ cup, or to taste
½ cup chopped onion
4 cloves garlic, finely chopped
2 cups ketchup
1/3 cup vinegar
3 tablespoons
Worcestershire sauce to taste
½ cup brown sugar, firmly packed
¾ cup molasses
½ teaspoon pepper
½ tablespoon salt
¼ cup tomato paste
1 teaspoon Liquid Smoke
½ teaspoon Tabasco sauce, or to taste

Combine onion, garlic and Jack Daniels in a 3 quart saucepan. Sauté until translucent, about 10 minutes. Add all remaining ingredients, bring to boil. Simmer uncovered until reduced and thickened, about 15 to 25 minutes.

## *Jim Beam Barbecue Sauce*

2 cups tomato ketchup
1 cup brown sugar, packed
3 tablespoons Worcestershire sauce
2 teaspoons dry mustard
1 cup Jim Beam Kentucky Straight Bourbon Whiskey
4 tablespoons cider vinegar
4 tablespoons soy sauce
1/2 teaspoon ground cayenne pepper
Dash liquid smoke, to taste, optional

Combine all ingredients in 2-quart saucepan. Bring to a boil over high heat, stirring occasionally. Reduce heat to low; simmer uncovered 20 minutes, or until thickened, stirring occasionally.

## North Carolina Vinegar Sauce

½ pound margarine
½ cup vinegar
Juice of 1 lemon
1 ½ tablespoons Worcestershire sauce
1 tablespoon honey
2 teaspoons salt
1 teaspoon black pepper

Melt margarine in a sauce pan. Add lemon juice, Worcestershire sauce, honey, salt and pepper. Bring to a boil. Remove from heat. Stir in vinegar and allow to cool

## *South Carolina Mustard Sauce*

1 cup yellow mustard
½ cup balsamic vinegar
1/3 cup brown sugar
2 tablespoons butter
1 tablespoon Worcestershire sauce
1 tablespoon lemon juice
1 teaspoon cayenne

Mix all ingredients together and simmer over a low heat for 30 minutes. If you are making this sauce for a whole hog multiple the ingredients by about 8.

# RUBS

## *Cajun Turkey Seasoning*

4 tablespoons salt
4 tablespoons ground onion powder
2 tablespoons ground garlic
2 tablespoons red pepper flakes

Mix ingredients together and rub over the entire surface of the turkey, inside and out. Let sit for about 2 hours.

## *Creole Turkey Rub*

25 whole bay leaves
3 tablespoons Creole seasoning
3 teaspoons dried thyme
3 teaspoons dried oregano
2 teaspoons garlic powder
1 1/2 teaspoons black pepper

Grind bay leaves into a fine powder. Combine all ingredients together. Divide into 3 equal parts. Rub one third on the inside of the turkey, one third over the breasts and one third over the rest of the turkey.

For best results refrigerate turkey overnight to allow the flavors to sink in.

## *Deep Fried Turkey Rub*

This recipe calls for a lot of bay leaves. It's actually about 1/3 cup, so if you have crushed bay leaves you can use that. The real secret to fried turkey is to get the rub well on the surface of the turkey before it hits the oil.

25 medium whole bay leaves
3 tablespoons hot Creole seasoning
3 teaspoons dried thyme
3 teaspoons dried oregano
2 teaspoons garlic powder
1 ½ teaspoons black peppercorns

In a spice grinder, grind the bay leaves into a fine powder. Place in small bowl. Grind thyme, oregano, peppercorns similarly. Add all ingredients to bowl and mix together. Divide into three equal parts.

Rub one part on the inside of turkey. Rub the second third under the skin around the breasts. And rub the last portion over the outside of the turkey. Refrigerate overnight.

## Herb Turkey Rub

This is a great rub for turkey anyway you plan to cook it. It really is best that you use fresh rosemary because you want the oils from the rosemary to season the turkey.

¼ cup white wine Worcestershire sauce
¼ cup olive oil
4 teaspoons fresh rosemary, chopped
4 teaspoons fresh thyme, chopped
4 teaspoons onion, minced
4 teaspoons garlic, minced
2 teaspoons salt

Combine all ingredients and mix well. Store in the refrigerator.

## Old Fashioned Turkey Rub

**When rubbing poultry you want to get it under the skin. Skin blocks flavor, and while you might get some tasty skin it won't help flavor the meat.**

1 tablespoon garlic powder
2 teaspoons seasoned salt
1 teaspoons poultry seasoning
1 teaspoon paprika
1 teaspoon salt
½ teaspoon pepper
¼ teaspoon cayenne pepper
¼ teaspoon basil

Combine all ingredients and store in an air tight container. Makes enough rub for a 20 pound turkey.

# VEGETABLES

—ɯ—

## *Bell Pepper Salad*

1 onion
2 red bell peppers
2 yellow bell peppers
3 tablespoons olive oil
2 large zucchini, sliced
2 garlic cloves, sliced
1 tablespoon balsamic vinegar
1 ¾ ounces anchovy fillets, chopped
¼ cup black olives, halved and pitted
1 tablespoon chopped fresh basil
Salt and pepper

**Tomato Toasts**
Small stick of French bread
1 garlic clove, crushed
1 tomato, peeled and chopped
2 tablespoons olive oil

Cut the onion into wedges. Core and de-seed the bell peppers and cut into thick slices.

Heat the oil in a large heavy-based skillet. Add the onion, bell peppers, zucchini, and garlic and fry gently for 20 minutes, stirring occasionally.

Add the vinegar, anchovies, olives, and seasoning to taste, mix thoroughly and leave to cool. Spoon onto individual plates and sprinkle with the basil.

To make the tomato toasts, cut the French bread diagonally into ½ inch slices. Mix the garlic, tomato, oil, and seasoning together, and spread thinly over each slice of bread.

Place the bread on a cookie sheet, drizzle with the olive oil and bake in a preheated oven, 425 degrees, for 5-10 minutes until crisp. Serve the Tomato Toasts with the bell pepper salad.

# Broccoli & Almond Salad

1 pound small broccoli flowerets
1 ¾ ounces baby corn-on-the-cobs, halved lengthwise
1 red bell pepper, seeded and cut into thin strips
1 ¾ ounces blanched almonds

**Dressing**
1 tablespoon sesame seeds
1 tablespoon peanut oil
2 garlic cloves, crushed
2 tablespoons light soy sauce
1 tablespoon honey
2 teaspoons lemon juice
Pepper
Lemon rind, to garnish (optional)

Spray grilling wok with non-stick cooking spray and grill the broccoli and baby corn cobs in a grilling wok 5 minutes. Transfer the broccoli and baby corn cobs to a large mixing bowl and add the bell pepper and almonds.

To make the dressing, heat a wok and add the sesame seeds. Dry-fry, stirring constantly, for about 1 minute, or until the sesame seeds are lightly browned and are giving off a delicious aroma.

Mix the peanut oil, garlic, soy sauce, honey, lemon juice, and pepper to taste. Add the sesame seeds and mix well.

Pour the dressing over the salad, cover, and set aside in the refrigerator for a minimum of 4 hours and preferably overnight.

Garnish the salad with lemon rind (if using) and serve.

## Campfire Grilled Cabbage

1 large head cabbage
1 ½ teaspoons garlic powder, or to taste
Salt and pepper to taste

Preheat grill for medium heat. Cut the cabbage into 8 wedges, and remove the core. Place all the wedges on a piece of aluminum foil large enough to wrap the cabbage. Season to taste with garlic powder, salt, and pepper. Seal cabbage in the foil.

Grill for 30 to 40 minutes on the preheated grill, until tender.

## Campfire Vidalias

4 Vidalia onions
4 tablespoons butter
4 cloves chopped garlic
Salt to taste
Peel onions, and cut each one into quarters, keeping onion together. Place one tablespoon of butter and one whole clove of garlic into the center of each one. Double wrap each onion in aluminum foil and drop into the hot coals of your campfire.

Cook for 30 to 40 minutes. Carefully remove them from the coals and tear them open. Season with salt to taste, and eat.

## *Char-Broiled Vegetables*

1 large red bell pepper
1 large green bell pepper
1 large orange bell pepper
1 large zucchini
4 baby eggplant
2 medium red onions
2 tablespoons lemon juice
1 tablespoon olive oil
1 garlic clove, crushed
1 tablespoon chopped, fresh rosemary or 1 teaspoon dried rosemary
Salt and pepper

Halve and de-seed the bell peppers and cut into even sized pieces, about 1-inch wide.

Trim the zucchini, cut in half lengthways, and slice into 1-inch pieces. Place the bell peppers and zucchini in a large bowl.

Trim the eggplant and quarter them lengthways. Peel both the onions, then cut each one into 8 even-sized wedges. Add the pieces of eggplant and onions to the bowl containing the wedges of bell peppers and zucchini.

In a small bowl, whisk together the lemon juice, olive oil, garlic, rosemary, and seasoning. Pour the mixture over the vegetables and stir to coat evenly.

Preheat the grill to medium. Thread the vegetables onto 8 metal or pre-soaked wooden skewers. Arrange the kabobs on the rack and cook for 10-12 minutes, turning frequently, until the vegetables are lightly charred and just softened.

Drain the vegetables and serve on a bed of cracked wheat accompanied by a tomato and olive relish.

## Cheese and Herb Stuffed Tomatoes

2 large firm tomatoes
3 tablespoons fresh white bread crumbs
2 tablespoons finely chopped fresh parsley
1 small garlic clove, crushed
1 ounce grated cheese; cheddar, mozzarella, etc.
2 tablespoons soft butter
A pinch of dried basil

Preheat the grill to medium heat. Cut the tomatoes in half lengthways and scrape out the seeds using a teaspoon. Combine the remaining ingredients and lightly pack the mixture into the tomato cavities. Place the tomato halves, cut side up, on the grill and cook, over medium heat, for about 10 minutes or until the tomatoes are heated through and the cheese has melted.

## Coleslaw

2/3 cup low-fat mayonnaise
2/3 cup low-fat plain yogurt
Dash of Tabasco sauce
1 medium head white cabbage
4 carrots
1 green bell pepper
2 tablespoons sunflower seeds
Salt and pepper

To make the dressing, combine the mayonnaise, yogurt, Tabasco sauce, and salt and pepper to taste in a small bowl. Leave to chill until required.

Cut the cabbage in half and then into quarters. Remove and discard the tough center stalk. Shred the cabbage leaves finely. Wash the leaves and dry them thoroughly.

Peel the carrots and shred using a food processor or mandolin. Alternatively, coarsely grate the carrot.

Quarter and de-seed the bell pepper and cut the flesh into thin strips.

Combine the vegetables in a large mixing bowl and toss to mix. Pour over the dressing and toss until the vegetables are well coated. Leave to chill in the refrigerator until required.

Just before serving, place the sunflower seeds on a cookie sheet and toast them in the oven or under the broiler until golden brown. Transfer the salad to a large serving dish, scatter with sunflower seeds, and serve.

## Crab Stuffed Grilled Mushrooms

1 cup crabmeat
½ cup cream cheese
½ cup fresh parsley leaves, chopped
½ cup green onions, chopped
4 tablespoons Parmesan House Seasoning, recipe follows
10 white mushrooms caps
½ cup bread crumbs
Nonstick cooking spray

Preheat the grill to medium heat. Combine the crabmeat, cream cheese, parsley, green onions and Parmesan. Season with House Seasoning, to taste. Stuff the mushroom caps with the mixture and top with bread crumbs. Spray the tops with nonstick spray to help them brown. Transfer to the grill and grill for about 20 minutes, or until the filling is hot and melted.

**House Seasoning**
1 cup salt
¼ cup black pepper
¼ cup garlic powder
Mix ingredients together and store in an airtight container for up to 6 months.

## *Dill-and-Almond Green Beans*

1 pound fresh green beans, trimmed
¼ cp slivered almonds
1 tablespoon olive oil
1 garlic clove, minced
1 tablespoon chopped fresh dill
½ teaspoon salt
½ teaspoon pepper

Cook beans in boiling water to cover in a Dutch oven over medium-high heat 10 minutes. Plunge into ice water to stop the cooking process; drain.

Sauté almonds in hot oil in a large skillet over medium heat 3 minutes or until lightly browned. Add garlic, sauté 30 seconds. Stir in green beans, dill, salt, and pepper; cook 2 minutes or until thoroughly heated. Serve immediately.

## *Easy-Delicious Parmesan Foil Potatoes*

Bag of frozen O'Brien Potatoes
¾ cup Pepper Parmesan Salad Dressing
1 ½ cups shredded cheddar cheese
Take two sheets of heavy duty aluminum foil. Place one sheet on top of the other and spray with non-stick cooking spray. Place the potatoes in a bowl and mix with the Pepper Parmesan Salad Dressing. Pour the mixture over the foil. Cover with cheese. Seal the foil, so that the foil does not touch the cheese.

Grill over medium heat for 25 minutes.

## Eight Jewel Vegetables

2 tablespoons peanut oil
6 scallions, sliced
3 garlic cloves, crushed
1 green bell pepper, seeded and diced
1 red bell pepper, seeded and diced
1 fresh red chili, sliced
2 tablespoons chopped water chestnuts
1 zucchini, chopped
4 ½ ounces oyster mushrooms
3 tablespoons black bean sauce
2 teaspoons Chinese rice wine or dry sherry
4 tablespoons dark soy sauce
1 teaspoon dark brown sugar
2 tablespoons water
1 teaspoon sesame oil

Heat the peanut oil in a preheated wok or large skillet until it is smoking. Lower the heat slightly, add the scallions and garlic, and stir-fry for about 30 seconds.

Add the red and green bell peppers, fresh red chili, water chestnuts, and zucchini to the wok or skillet and stir-fry for 2-3 minutes, or until the vegetables are just beginning to soften.

Add the oyster mushrooms, black bean sauce. Chinese rice wine of dry sherry, dark soy sauce, dark brown sugar, and water to the wok and stir-fry for 4 minutes more.

Sprinkle the stir-fry with sesame oil and serve immediately.

## Fancy Grilled Green Beans

2 tablespoons teriyaki sauce
1 tablespoon honey
1 tablespoon butter
1 tablespoon fresh lemon juice
1 ½ pounds fresh green beans
2 slices bacon
½ cup red bell pepper strips
½ cup thin onion wedges
½ cup whole cashews

In a small bowl, stir together the teriyaki sauce, honey, and butter.

Fill a bowl with cold water and ice cubes.
Bring a large pot of water to a boil and add the lemon juice. Drop in the beans and cook for 4 to 5 minutes, or until beans are bright green. Drain the beans in a colander and then plunge them into the iced water. Drain again and set aside.

In a skillet, cook the bacon until very crispy, crumble and set aside. Sauté the bell pepper and onion in the hot bacon fat for 2 minutes. Add the beans, cashews, and bacon to the skillet. Add the teriyaki-honey sauce and toss gently.

## *Field Pea and Corn Salad*

2 ears corn, shucked
½ medium red onion
1 cup cooked field peas
½ cup seeded diced red tomato
½ cup seeded diced green tomato
1 teaspoon finely minced shallot
1 teaspoon chopped basil
1 teaspoon chopped chives
1 teaspoon chopped flat-leaf parsley
1 teaspoon red wine vinegar
1 teaspoon sherry vinegar
2 tablespoons olive oil
Kosher salt and freshly ground black pepper to taste

Cook the corn in unsalted boiling water for 3 minutes; drain. Place the corn directly on a hot grill and cook, turning occasionally, until charred. Let cool, then slice off the kernels. Grill the onion cut side down until charred. Let cool, then chop.

Combine the corn, onion, and all the remaining ingredients in a large bowl and toss to mix well. Let the flavors marry for an hour in the refrigerator. Bring to room temperature before serving.

## *Foil Wrapped Campfire Veggies*

2 ½ pounds new potatoes, thinly sliced
1 large sweet potato, thinly sliced
2 Vidalia onions, sliced ¼ -inch thick
½ pound fresh green beans, cut into 1-inch pieces
1 sprig fresh rosemary
1 sprig fresh thyme
2 tablespoons olive oil
Salt and pepper to taste
¼ cup olive oil

Preheat grill for high heat. In a large bowl, combine the new potatoes, sweet potato, Vidalia onions, green beans, rosemary, and thyme. Stir in 2 tablespoons olive oil, salt, and pepper to coat.

Using 2 to 3 layers of foil, create desired number of foil packets. Brush inside surfaces of packets liberally with remaining olive oil. Distribute vegetable mixture evenly among the packets. Seal tightly.

Place packets on the preheated grill. Cook 30 minutes, turning once, or until potatoes are tender.

## Fresh Green Beans with Bacon Dressing

½ pound green beans, trimmed
2 bacon slices, cooked and chopped
1 tablespoon chopped shallot
2 teaspoons white wine vinegar

Grill oiled green beans over medium heat until tender, about
8 minutes, turning once. Cut green beans into 2-inch lengths.
Transfer to shallow bowl. Combine bacon, shallot and vinegar.
Pour over the green beans and toss.

## Grilled Apples and Sweet Potatoes

2 medium apples, cored and cut into eighths
2 medium sweet potatoes, peeled and cut into one inch cubes
¼ cup maple syrup
¼ teaspoon ground cinnamon
¼ teaspoon salt
¼ teaspoon black pepper

Cook sweet potatoes in boiling water for 10 minutes and drain.
Place sweet potatoes and apples in an 18-inch square sheet of
heavy-duty aluminum foil. In a small bowl, mix other ingredients
and pour over the potatoes and apples.

Seal the aluminum foil, but leave room for steam to build.
Place foil packet over medium heat and grill for twenty-five
minutes.

## Grilled Cajun Potato Wedges

3 large russet potatoes, washed and scrubbed (do not peel)
¼ cup olive oil
2 cloves garlic, minced
1 teaspoon salt
1 teaspoon paprika
½ teaspoon dried thyme leaves
½ teaspoon dried oregano leaves
¼ teaspoon black pepper
1/8 to ¼ teaspoon ground red pepper
2 cups mesquite wood chips

Cut potatoes in half lengthwise; then cut each half lengthwise into 4 wedges. Place potatoes in large bowl. Add oil and garlic; toss to coat well.

Combine salt, paprika, thyme, oregano, black pepper, and ground red pepper in small bowl. Sprinkle over potatoes; toss to coat well. Place potato wedges in single layer in shallow roasting pan. Reserve remaining oil mixture.

Bake at 425 degrees for 20 minutes.

Meanwhile, cover mesquite chips with cold water; soak 20 minutes. Drain mesquite chips; sprinkle over coals or place in a smoker box for your gas grill. Place potato wedges on their sides on grid. Grill potato wedges, on covered grill, over medium heat 15 to 20 minutes or until potatoes are browned and fork-tender, brushing with reserved oil mixture halfway through grilling time and turning once with tongs.

## Great Grilled Vegetables

1 small eggplant
1 small zucchini
1 Cubanelle (light green) Italian pepper
1 small red onion
8 medium crimini mushrooms (Baby portabellas)
½ cup extra-virgin olive oil
Salt and Pepper to taste
2 tablespoons chopped fresh thyme

Preheat grill or grill pan over moderate to high heat. Assemble cut veggies on a platter; as you place them on the grill, brush each side with a little oil and season with salt and pepper. Cook until are just tender, 3 to 5 minutes on each side, depending on the vegetable. Arrange grilled veggies on a platter and garnish with a generous sprinkle of chopped fresh thyme.

## Grilled Hash brown Casserole

1 bag of ORE-IDA Frozen Hash browns (defrosted) or "Potatoes
O'Brien" w/onion & bell pepper
8 ounces of sour cream
1 can cream of mushroom soup
16 ounces shredded cheddar cheese
1 stick of butter (melted)

Mix all ingredients in a large bowl (save ½ of cheddar cheese) and
place in iron skillet sprayed with Pam. Sprinkle with remaining
cheese. Cook over the grill on medium heat for 30 to 40 minutes.

## *Grilled Jumbo Asparagus with Egg and Herb Vinaigrette*

16 jumbo asparagus spears, tough ends cut away and bottom half peeled
4 hard-boiled eggs, peeled and finely chopped
¼ cup Sherry Vinaigrette
1/3 cup coarsely chopped chives, flat-leaf parsley, and tarragon
Kosher salt and freshly ground black pepper
Olive oil for brushing

Bring a large saucepan of salted water to a boil. Add the asparagus and cook until just tender, about 4 minutes. Drain and blot dry on a kitchen towel.

In a medium bowl, combine the eggs, vinaigrette, and all but 1 tablespoon of the herbs. Season with salt and pepper.

Brush the grill with a little olive oil. Place the asparagus spears on the hot grill and brush with olive oil. Grill, turning occasionally, until lightly charred, about 4 minutes total.

Divide the asparagus among serving plates. Spoon a fat ribbon of the vinaigrette over each plate of asparagus. Garnish with a scattering of the remaining herbs.

**Sherry Vinaigrette:**
½ shallot, finely minced
4 thyme sprigs, leaves removed
2 tablespoons sherry vinegar
6 tablespoons extra virgin olive oil
Kosher salt and freshly ground black pepper to taste

In a small bowl, combine the shallot, thyme, and a good pinch each of salt and pepper. Add the sherry vinegar and let macerate for 10 minutes. Whisk in the olive oil in a slow steady stream. Taste and adjust the seasoning. (The vinaigrette can be refrigerated for up to 5 days.)

## Grilled Mashed Potatoes with Parmesan Cheese and Bread Crumbs

1 tablespoon butter
4 pounds russet potatoes, peeled, cut into 1-inch pieces
1 cup whole milk
½ cup (1 stick) butter, melted
1 ½ cups grated mozzarella
1 cup freshly grated Parmesan
Salt and freshly ground black pepper
2 tablespoons plain dry bread crumbs

Preheat the grill to medium high heat. Coat a cast iron skillet with 1 tablespoon of butter and set aside.

Cook the potatoes in a large pot of boiling salted water until they are very tender, about 15 minutes. Drain; return the potatoes to the same pot and mash well. Mix in the milk and melted butter. Mix in the mozzarella and 3/4 cup of the Parmesan. Season to taste with salt and pepper. Transfer the potatoes to the prepared cast iron skillet. Stir the bread crumbs and remaining ¼ cup of Parmesan in a small bowl to blend. Sprinkle the bread crumb mixture over the mashed potatoes. Recipe can be prepared up to this point 6 hours ahead of time; cover and chill.

Grill, uncovered, until the topping is golden brown, about 20 minutes.

## Grilled Sweet Potatoes

4 medium sweet potatoes
½ cup melted butter
3 tablespoons brown sugar
1 teaspoon ground cinnamon

Cut sweet potatoes into ¾-inch slices. Bring 3 quarts of water to a boil and add potatoes. Simmer until potatoes are just starting to soften. Cool and peal. Combine butter, brown sugar and cinnamon, brush over potatoes.

Place potato slices on preheated grill and cook, turning once until potatoes begin to brown.

## Grilled Sweet Potato Casserole

2 ½ pounds sweet potatoes (about 3 large), scrubbed
2 large eggs, lightly beaten with a fork
3 tablespoons unsalted butter, melted plus more for the preparing the pan
2 tablespoons packed dark brown sugar
1 teaspoon kosher salt
½ teaspoon ground cinnamon
½ teaspoon ground ginger
Pinch of freshly grated nutmeg
Freshly ground black pepper
¼ cup coarsely chopped pecans

Preheat the oven to medium high heat. Put the sweet potatoes on a baking sheet and pierce each one 2-3 times with a fork. Grill for 45 to 60 minutes or until tender. Set aside to cool.

Turn the grill down to medium. Scoop the sweet potato out of their skins and into a medium bowl. Discard the skins. Mash the potatoes until smooth. Add the eggs, butter, brown sugar, salt, cinnamon, ginger, nutmeg, and pepper to taste. Whisk the mixture until smooth.

Butter a cast iron skillet. Pour the sweet potato mixture into the skillet and sprinkle the top with the pecans. Grill for 30 to 40 minutes until a bit puffy.

## Grilled Tomato Peppers

2 large yellow bell peppers
8 cherry tomatoes, halved
1 tablespoon olive oil
¼ teaspoon garlic salt
¼ teaspoon black pepper
½ cup feta cheese
2 tablespoons chopped basil

Cut peppers in halves and remove the seeds. Grill pepper halves, cut side down for five minutes. Turn. Place four tomato halves in each pepper pocket. Brush with olive oil, sprinkle with garlic salt and black pepper. Grill 4 more minutes.

Sprinkle tomatoes with cheese. Grill 2 more minutes or until cheese is melted. Remove from grill and sprinkle with basil.

## Grilled Tarragon Potato Salad

2 slices Canadian bacon, thinly sliced
¼ cup olive oil
¼ cup vinegar
1 tablespoon sugar
¼ teaspoon dried, crushed tarragon
½ teaspoon Dijon mustard
1 pound tiny new potatoes, cut into bite sized pieces
1 cup chopped bok choy
½ cup chopped radishes
½ cup thinly sliced green onions
1 teaspoon black pepper

In a small bowl, combine olive oil, sugar, mustard, and tarragon. Mix well and set aside.

Spray potatoes with nonstick cooking spray. Wrap in heavy-duty aluminum foil and grill over medium heat for twenty-five minutes.

In a large bowl, combine potatoes, bok choy, radishes, green onions, Canadian bacon, and pepper. Add dressing and toss.

## Grilled Vidalia Onions

1 large Vidalia onion for each person
½ teaspoon butter for each onion

I keep it simple by just washing the onions, taking off excess skin, and cutting a hole large enough to hold the ½ teaspoon of butter. Wrap the onions in aluminum foil and cook along with the meat for not more than two hours.

If you want a little more flavor, just sprinkle a little of your "secret" rub recipe in the middle with the butter. I also pour a little chicken broth in the hole from time to time.

## *Herby Potatoes & Onion*

2 pounds waxy potatoes cut into cubes
½ cup butter
1 red onion, cut into 8
2 garlic cloves, crushed
1 teaspoon lemon juice
2 tablespoons chopped thyme
Salt and pepper

Cook the cubed potatoes in a saucepan of boiling water for 10 minutes. Drain thoroughly.

Melt the butter in a large, heavy-bottomed skillet and add the red onion wedges, garlic, and lemon juice. Cook, stirring constantly for 2-3 minutes. Add the potatoes to the pan and mix well to coat in the butter mixture.

Reduce the heat, cover, and cook for 25-30 minutes, or until the potatoes are golden brown and tender. Sprinkle the chopped thyme over the top of the potatoes and season.

Transfer to a warm serving dish and serve immediately.

## Italian Grilled Corn

8 ears of fresh corn, shucked
8 sheets of paper towels
8 sheets of heavy duty aluminum foil, cut a little large than the paper towels
1 bottle of Zesty Italian Salad Dressing
Lay a paper towel on top of each sheet of aluminum foil. Salt and pepper each paper towel. Squirt Italian salad dressing all over each paper towel, just enough to make it wet.

Place an ear of corn on top of each paper towel. Roll the paper towel up. Then, roll the paper towel and corn up in the sheet of aluminum foil.

Grill over medium heat for twenty-five minutes, turning every five minutes.

## *Mixed Wild Mushroom and Parmigiano Salad*

### Dressing
3 to 4 tablespoons extra virgin olive oil
1 to 2 tablespoons balsamic vinegar or red wine vinegar

### Salad
5 ounces assorted mushrooms (morels, crimini, shiitaki, chanterelles)
Salt and freshly ground pepper
4 to 5 fresh basil leaves, finely shredded or minced or 1 teaspoon minced fresh parsley
1 ounce thinly sliced Parmigiano-Reggiano

In a small bowl, whisk together the oil and vinegar and set aside.

Wipe mushrooms clean with a damp cloth, cut them into thin slices and place in a medium bowl. Season the mushrooms with salt and a little pepper, toss with basil or parsley and the dressing. Taste and adjust the seasoning.

Arrange in small mounds on serving plates, top with sliced Parmigiano and serve.

Can make ahead, preparing the dressing and mushrooms. Assemble the salad just before serving.

## Oven Steak Fries

5 Russet potatoes
3 tablespoons extra-virgin olive oil
1 teaspoon dried thyme
1 teaspoon dried oregano
1 tablespoon Montreal Seasoning

Preheat grill to medium-high. Spray a grilling sheet with non-stick cooking spray. Cut potatoes and spread out on the grilling sheet. Coat potatoes with olive oil, dried herbs, and steak seasoning or salt and pepper. Spread potatoes evenly over the grilling sheet, place on the grill and grill for 25 minutes, turning them once, halfway in the grilling process. Serve fries hot from the grill.

## *Parchment Potatoes*

For each serving:

12 x 12-inch piece baking parchment paper
3 small red potatoes, quartered
3 cloves garlic
¼ small onion, thinly sliced
2 teaspoons olive oil
Sprig of fresh Rosemary (or 1 teaspoon dry)
Salt and pepper to taste
1 tablespoon Parmesan cheese

Fold the paper diagonally. Crease it then open up again. Put potatoes, onions and garlic on paper, center it next to the crease.

Add rosemary, salt and pepper. Sprinkle 1 tablespoon parmesan on top. Drizzle oil over all and fold packet edges so that they are tightly rolled and the finished packet looks like a half-round.

Bake 45 minutes on a cookie sheet at 350 degrees. Serve on bread and butter-size plates as a side dish.

Before serving, cut an "X" in the top of the packet and open slightly. Let each guest open packets completely.

## Pasta with Green Vegetables

2 cups gemelli or other pasta shapes
1 tablespoon olive oil
2 tablespoons chopped fresh parsley
2 tablespoons freshly grated Parmesan cheese
Salt and pepper

**Sauce**
1 head of green broccoli, cut into flowerets
2 zucchini, sliced
8 ounces asparagus spears, trimmed
4 ½ ounces snow peas
1 cup frozen peas
2 tablespoons butter
3 tablespoons vegetable stock
5 tablespoons heavy cream
Large pinch of freshly grated nutmeg

Cook the pasta in a large pan of salted boiling water, adding the olive oil, for 8-10 minutes or until tender. Drain the pasta in a colander, return to the pan, cover, and keep warm.

Steam the broccoli, zucchini, asparagus spears, and snow peas over a pan of boiling, salted water until just beginning to soften. Remove from the heat and plunge into cold water to prevent further cooking. Drain thoroughly and set aside.

Cook the peas in boiling, salted water for 3 minutes, then drain. Refresh in cold water and drain again.

Put the butter and vegetable stock in a pan over medium heat. Add all of the vegetables, except the asparagus spears, and toss carefully with a wooden spoon to heat through, taking care not to break them up. Stir in the cream, allow the sauce to heat through and season with salt, pepper, and nutmeg.

Transfer the pasta to a warm serving dish and stir in the chopped parsley. Spoon the sauce over, and sprinkle on the freshly grated Parmesan. Arrange the asparagus spears in a pattern on top. Serve hot.

## *Portobello Burgers with Green Sauce and Smoked Mozzarella*

2 tablespoons extra-virgin olive oil
4 large Portobello mushroom caps
Steak seasoning blend
¼ cup balsamic vinegar
½ pound fresh smoked mozzarella cheese, sliced

**Green Sauce**
1 cup loosely packed basil leaves
½ cup fresh flat-leaf parsley leaves
3 tablespoons capers
1 cove garlic
The juice of ½ lemon
¼ cup extra-virgin olive oil
Salt and freshly ground black pepper, to taste
½ cup grated Parmigiano Reggiano or Romano cheese
½ medium red onion, thinly sliced
4 leaves romaine or red leaf lettuce

Heat the grill to medium-high heat. Add oiled mushroom caps. Season mushrooms with steak seasoning blend or salt and pepper, and grill 3 minutes on each side. Baste the mushrooms with vinegar. Turn mushrooms cap side up and cover with sliced cheese. Turn off heat and cover pan with foil. Let stand 2 or 3 minutes for cheese to melt.

To make the sauce, combine basil, parsley, capers, garlic, and lemon juice in the food processor. Pulse grind, until finely chopped and scrape into a bowl. Stir in oil, salt, pepper, and cheese.

Slather bun tops with green sauce. Pile portabellas on bun bottoms and top with red onion slices and lettuce.

## *Potatoes in Italian Dressing*

1 pound 10 ounces waxy potatoes
1 shallot
2 tomatoes
1 tablespoon chopped fresh basil
Salt

**Italian Dressing**
1 tomato, peeled and chopped finely
4 black olives, pitted and chopped finely
4 tablespoons olive oil
1 tablespoon wine vinegar
1 garlic clove, crushed
Salt and pepper

Grill the potatoes in grilling wok for twenty-five minutes or until they are tender. Drain the potatoes well, chop roughly, and put into a bowl.
Chop the shallot. Cut the tomatoes into wedges and add the shallot and tomatoes to the potatoes.

To make the dressing, put all the ingredients into a screw-top jar and mix together thoroughly. Pour the dressing over the potato mixture and toss thoroughly.

Transfer the salad to a serving dish and sprinkle with the basil.

## Risotto-Stuffed Bell Peppers

4 red or orange bell peppers
1 tablespoon olive oil
1 large onion, finely chopped
1 2/3 cups risotto rice, washed
About 15 strands of saffron
2/3 cup white wine
3 ¾ cups hot vegetable or chicken stock
3 tablespoons butter
2/3 cup grated pecorino cheese
1 ¾ ounces Italian sausage, such as Felino salami or other coarse
Italian salami, chopped
7 ounces mozzarella cheese, sliced

Cut the bell peppers in half, retaining some of the stalk. Remove
the seeds. Place the bell peppers, cut side up, under a preheated
broiler for 12-15 minutes or until softened and charred.

Meanwhile, heat the oil in a large skillet. Add the onion and cook
for 3-4 minutes or until softened. Add the rice and saffron, stirring
to coat in the oil, and cook for 1 minute.

Add the white wine and hot stock gradually, one ladleful at a time,
making sure that all of the liquid has been absorbed before adding
the next ladleful of liquid. When all of the liquid is absorbed, the
rice should be cooked and tender. Test by tasting a grain, if it is still
crunchy, add a little more water and continue cooking. It should
take at least 15 minutes to cook.

Stir in the butter, pecorino cheese, and the chopped Italian sausage.

Spoon the risotto into the bell peppers. Top with a slice of mozzarella and broil for 4-5 minutes or until the cheese is bubbling.
Serve hot.

# Sausage and Spinach-Stuffed Mushrooms

1 tablespoon extra-virgin olive oil
12 large white gourmet stuffing mushroom caps, stems removed
for stuffing, brushed with damp towel
Salt and freshly ground black pepper, to taste

**Stuffing**
1 ½ teaspoons extra-virgin olive oil
¾ pound sweet bulk Italian sausage
12 stems of mushrooms, finely chopped
2 cloves garlic, finely chopped
1 rib of celery and green, leafy top from the heart of the stalk,
chopped
½ small onion, chopped
½ small red bell pepper, seeded and chopped
1 box (10 oz.) chopped frozen spinach, defrosted and squeezed dry
2 slices white toasting bread, toasted and buttered, chopped into
small dice
¼ cup grated Parmigiano Reggiano or Romano cheese

Heat the grill at medium-high heat. Spray mushroom caps with
nonstick cooking spray and season with salt and pepper. Grill 5 to
7 minutes, turning once, until they are lightly browned and tender
at edges. Turn caps topside up to let juices drain away. Transfer
caps to a small nonstick baking sheet.

In a skillet, add a touch of oil and the sausage to the hot skillet.
Brown and crumble sausage for 3 minutes, then add chopped
mushroom stems, garlic, celery, onion, and bell pepper. Sauté over
medium-heat, another 3 to 5 minutes. Add spinach and stir into
stuffing. Add bread cubes and cheese and toss until bread is moist
and stuffing is combined, 2 or 3 minutes.

Fill caps with stuffing using a small scoop or large spoon. Place
on a medium hot grill. Grill 6-8 minutes to crisp edges of stuffing.
Transfer to a serving plate.

## Smoked Baked Beans

1 #10 can of Bush's Original Baked Beans
1 medium onion, diced
1 cup of syrup
¾ cup of barbecue sauce.

Drain the beans. Add onion, syrup and barbecue sauce. Cover with foil. Smoke at 250 degrees for two hours.

## Southwestern Stuffed Peppers

1 cup of cooked white rice
2 long mild chili peppers, red or green
1 small onion, chopped
1 cup frozen peas
1 cup mild or medium taco sauce
Salt and Pepper to taste
2 tablespoons chopped cilantro or fresh flat-leaf parsley, for garnish
2 scallions, thinly sliced, for garnish

Slice peppers in half, lengthwise. Remove the seed pods. Spray with nonstick cooking spray and grill over medium heat for two minutes on each side. Remove from grill and allow to cool

In a separate bowl, combine rice, chopped onion, peas, taco sauce, salt, and pepper. Scoop the filling into the center of each pepper. Place peppers back on the grill and heat for two minutes. Serve with garnish of cilantro and scallions

## Stir-Fried Asparagus with Garlic

2 pounds asparagus
8 garlic cloves, finely chopped
2 tablespoons canola oil
3 tablespoons soy sauce

Snap tough ends off asparagus; discard ends. Cut asparagus in half.

Sauté asparagus and garlic in hot oil in a large skillet over medium-high heat on the grill for 3 to 5 minutes or until asparagus is crisp-tender. Add soy sauce; reduce heat to medium low, and cover. Cook 5 minutes or until asparagus is tender.

## *Stir Grilled Vegetables*

2 yellow squash
2 zucchini squash
10 small mushrooms
2 medium onions
½ cup Mr. BBQ's Magic Marinade

Wash and slice all of the vegetables. Marinate in Mr. BBQ's Magic Meat Marinade for thirty minutes. Place in a grill wok and sauté for ten minutes, stirring often.

## Stovetop Rosemary Potatoes

1 tablespoon virgin olive oil
2 cloves minced garlic
1 pound new potatoes, about 4 large ones, cut into 1-inch pieces
¼ teaspoon salt
¼ teaspoon pepper
1 teaspoon dried rosemary; crumbled

In a large non-stick skillet, heat oil. Add garlic and sauté about five
minutes. Cut potatoes into 1-inch pieces. Add to garlic and sprinkle
with salt, pepper and rosemary. Toss. Increase heat to medium,
cover and cook about 15 minutes. Recover and cook until potatoes
are browned, about 4 minutes.

## Vegetable Jambalaya

½ cup brown rice
2 tablespoons olive oil
2 garlic cloves, crushed
1 red onion, cut into eights
1 eggplant, diced
1 green bell pepper, diced
1 ¾ ounces baby corn-on-the-cobs, halved lengthwise
½ cup frozen peas
3 ½ ounces small broccoli flowerets
2/3 cup vegetable stock
8 ounces can chopped tomatoes
1 tablespoon tomato paste
1 teaspoon Creole seasoning
½ teaspoon chili flakes
Salt and pepper

Cook the rice in a large saucepan of salted boiling water for 20 minutes, or until cooked through. Drain, rinse with boiling water, drain again, and set aside.

Heat the oil in a heavy-bottomed skillet and cook the garlic and onion, stirring constantly, for 2-3 minutes.

Add the eggplant, bell pepper, corn, peas, and broccoli to the pan and cook, stirring occasionally, for 2-3 minutes. Stir in the vegetable stock and canned tomatoes, tomato paste, Creole seasoning, and chili flakes.

Season to taste and cook over a low heat for 15-20 minutes, or until the vegetables are tender.

Stir the brown rice into the vegetable mixture and cook, mixing well, for 3-4 minutes, or until hot. Transfer the vegetable jambalaya to a warm serving dish and serve immediately.

## Vegetable Pasta Stir-Fry

4 2/3 cups dried whole wheat pasta shells, or other short pasta
shapes
1 tablespoon olive oil
2 carrots, thinly sliced
4 ounces baby corn-on-the-cobs
3 tablespoons peanut oil
1-inch piece fresh ginger, thinly sliced
1 large onion, thinly sliced
1 garlic clove, thinly sliced
3 celery stalks, thinly sliced
1 small red bell pepper, seeded and sliced into thin strips
Salt
Steamed snow peas, to serve

**Sauce**
1 teaspoon cornstarch
2 tablespoons water
3 tablespoons soy sauce
3 tablespoons dry sherry
1 teaspoon honey
Dash or hot pepper sauce (optional)

Cook the pasta in a large pan of boiling lightly salted water, adding
the tablespoon of olive oil. When tender, but still firm to the bite,
drain the pasta in a colander, return to the pan, cover, and keep
warm.

Heat the peanut oil in a large grilling wok over medium heat. Add
the ginger and stir-fry for 1 minute, to flavor the oil. Remove with
a perforated spoon and discard. Grill the rest of the vegetables in a
solid grilling wok over medium heat for five minutes, and then stir
in the reserved pasta.

Put the cornstarch in a small bowl and mix to a smooth paste with
the water. Stir in the soy sauce, sherry, and honey. Pour the sauce

into the wok, stir well, and cook for 2 minutes, stirring once or twice. Taste the sauce and season with hot pepper sauce if you wish. Serve with a steamed green vegetable, such as snow peas.

# God's Plan for Your Salvation

—m—

1. Do you believe in God?
2. Do you believe that God loves you?
3. Do you believe that Jesus Christ is the Son of God? (John 20:31)
4. Do you believe that you are a sinner? (Romans 3:23)
5. Do you believe that Jesus Christ died for your sins? (Romans 5:8; 1 Timothy 1:15)
6. Do you want Jesus Christ to save you from your sins? (Romans 6:23)

Jesus said, *"I am the way, the truth, and the life: no man comes unto the Father, but by me."* John 14:6

The Bible says: *"If you shall confess with your mouth the Lord Jesus Christ and shall believe in your heart that God has raised Him from the dead, you shall be saved."*

*"For whosoever shall call upon the name of the Lord shall be saved."* Romans 10:9-13

7. Do you believe this?
8. Jesus Christ is God's only Son. Are you willing to call upon Him so yor sins will be forgiven?
9. You can receive Christ into your heart if you repeat a prayer like this and trust in Him as expressed in this prayer.

## An Example of Prayer

*Dear Lord,* I know I have done wrong and need forgiveness. Thank you for dying for my sins and for offering me eternal life. Please forgive me of my sins and help me turn from them. I now confess you as my Savior. Thane control of my life and help me live for Jesus. Thank you for coming into my life and giving me eternal life.

In Jesus name I pray. Amen.

10. Now that you have prayed, do you believe that Jesus Christ has forgiven you and saved you from your sins? (John 1:12)

# Chris Hughes Biographical Sketch

—⚏—

B arbecue isn't just a hobby for Chris Hughes. It is a passion. Chris Hughes traveled the world to hone his barbecue skills. Chris Hughes is a Professional Barbecue Judge and former Pit Boss for one of the Top Ten Professional Barbecue Cooking Teams in the World.

Chris Hughes parlayed his skills into a very successful catering business that has catered for thousands. Chris has barbecued for many national figures, including politicians, presidential candidates, Southern Gospel Sensations – *The Legacy Five*, and Lee Greenwood.

Chris Hughes has authored three grilling books, is a grilling columnist for the *Northwest Florida Daily News* and has been seen on the *Food Network* and the *Travel Channel*. Chris Hughes is the host of his own television shows: *Simply Grilling with Chris Hughes and On the Grill with Mr. BBQ*. Chris Hughes is a weekly feature on the national radio show, *The Max Howell Show*.